New Context
Student's Workbook

Chapter One
All in the Family 2

Chapter Two
Youth Culture 7

Chapter Three
Science and Technology 14

Chapter Four
Our Fragile Planet 23

Chapter Five
A Global Marketplace 30

Chapter Six
Inform, Educate and Entertain . 37

Chapter Seven
Turning Conflict into Art 44

Chapter Eight
The UK – Redefining a Nation? . 50

Chapter Nine
We the People 57

Chapter Ten
Who Am I? 64

Chapter Eleven
Moving Out 71

Self-Assessment Sheets 79

Acknowledgements 95

Dear Student,

The aim of this Workbook is to help improve your command of the vocabulary and structures in the *New Context – Student's Book* (SB). It offers a wide range of exercises which are closely linked to the texts in the SB. The grammar dealt with in the 'Watch Your Language' sections and many of the skills covered in the chapters are also reinforced in the Workbook. To give you additional help we have included references to the Skills Pages, the Glossary, and the relevant sections of the *Cornelsen English Grammar*. The separate key which is provided allows you in many cases to check your answers to the more controlled exercises. An additional innovation is the Self-Assessment Sheets, which should be used together with the Introduction in the SB.

The mix of controlled exercises and more open-ended, creative tasks is designed not only to improve your English but also to get you to think about the topics covered in the SB. However, we hope that the Workbook will be not just work but fun as well. So on these pages you will, we hope, feel sorry for the turkey whose young life was cut short at Thanksgiving. You will find out why English-speakers think of sex when Axel Schmidt talks about people being 'on the job'. The Workbook will also tell you how 'Old Macdonald Had a Farm' began life as a protest song. What's more, you can work out what your ideal partner would be like and help Supermacho get over his identity crisis ...

Geoff Sammon, Bonn

Exercise 1

➤ Working with Pictures (SB, p. 223)

Describing a Picture

➤ Lead-in, SB, p. 20

Complete the sentences below according to your own impressions of the painting by Norman Rockwell (SB, p. 21). Remember to say where in the picture the various elements are situated, i.e. centre, foreground, background, left, right.

The main focus of the painting appears to be ______________________________

____

The eye then moves to ______________________________

____

Finally, we see ______________________________

____

The perspective and the way the elements are arranged in the picture gives us the feeling

that ______________________________

____

Exercise 2

⚠ **Trouble spot**
Do not use the phrase *in former times* – it refers to a period much further back in time.

Talking about the Past

➤ Lead-in, SB, p. 20

Ask your grandparents or parents what life in a family was like when they were young. Write about five sentences. You may find the following phrases useful:

when he/she was a boy/girl • in those days • at that time • he/she used to • back then

Exercise 3

➤ Indirect Speech (*Cornelsen English Grammar*, §§ 273–280)

Overhearing a Conversation

➤ Text 1, SB, pp. 22 and 25

You are sitting on the bus listening to a conversation between two women who are talking about a friend of yours, Yvonne. One of the women is Yvonne's mother. Later you tell Yvonne what you heard. The first part has been done for you.

This is what they said:
'I'm having lots of problems with Yvonne. She's so secretive that she won't even tell me who she's going out with at night. And she isn't very sensible, either. She's got in with the wrong crowd, I'm afraid. I'm worried that she might get pregnant. Yvonne's so unreasonable, you know. I've tried to discuss it sensibly with her so that we can work out a solution together but she just won't listen.'
'Yes, young people today are very rebellious. Parents need to be strict – it's the only solution.'

And this is what you tell Yvonne:
Yvonne, you'll never guess what I overheard the other day. Your mother was talking about you with a friend. I heard it all when I was sitting behind them on the bus. Your Mum said ...

Describing Trends

➤ Text 3, SB, p. 28

Exercise 4

➤ Working with Numbers (SB, p. 226)

a Using the statistics in Text 3, describe three ways in which US society changed between 1990 and 2000.

1 ______________________________

____

____

2 ______________________________

____

____

3 ______________________________

____

____

b Look at the cartoons by the British cartoonist Posy Simmonds. Comment on attitudes to marriage in the past as they are depicted here and explain briefly how attitudes have changed.

➤ Working with Cartoons (SB, p. 225)

heving, merry, Berry, demn: *the substitution of 'e' for 'a' in these words is a parody of old-fashioned standard English pronunciation*

Exercise 5

Family Backgrounds

➤ Text 2, SB, p. 26

Using the Internet or other reference works, find out about the family background of a famous person either living or dead, for example details about their childhood. Give the rest of the class a brief summary and let them guess who the famous person is or was. Use the guide below to make brief notes.

Born (date and place): ______________________________

____

Occupation: ______________________________

____

Parents' occupations: ______________________________

____

Family situation: ______________________________

____

Childhood experiences: ______________________________

____

Other details: ______________________________

____

____

Exercise 6

Family Types

➤ Lead-in, Text 3, SB, pp. 20, 28

Choose one of the family types illustrated in the cartoons below. Write a short imaginative description (about 100 words) giving details of the family and answering the questions. The vocabulary you collected for task 1a on p. 20 of the SB may help you.

1 What are the names of the family members?
2 How long have they been a family?
3 Main events in the family history (e.g. children born or adopted, separation, divorce).

Is This What I Died for?

➤ Text 4A, SB, p. 31

Exercise 7

The turkey in Text 4A is in Turkey Heaven, looking down sadly on the Anderson family's attempts to make Thanksgiving dinner. Fill in the gaps with suitable words or phrases from the text so that they fit the numbered clues given below.

It really makes me sick to see people like the Andersons. There are people in the developing world who are ____________ (1), and the Andersons are wasting a delicious plump turkey like me. The mother's hopeless. My poor dead body is still ____________ (2) because she forgot to ____________ (3) me the night before, so she puts me in hot water! Then she hacks at my ____________ (4) with an ice pick. It hurts just to think about it! Dad has a go next. He tries to chop my poor dead body into smaller pieces with the ____________ (5), but it sticks in my flesh. So he ________ (6) me! What does he think I am – a piece of wood? He needs his eyes examined! Of course he drops the meat on the ground. So what does he do? Washes it in the ________ (7) with ____________ (8)! To add insult to injury he decides to make ________ (9) out of me. Has he no shame? I'm a turkey of quality and breeding. My ancestors were here before the Pilgrim Fathers. Is this what I died for? I'm wasted on the Andersons. They've really ____________ (10) this time. Oh well, at least my body gets ____________ (11) decently, next to their dog.

(1) die of hunger
(2) ice-cold and hard
(3) defrost sth. (e.g. food)
(4) organs in and around an animal's stomach
(5) small axe
(6) use a saw (= Säge)
(7) place in the kitchen where you wash things
(8) liquid or powder which helps to remove dirt, e.g. when doing the dishes
(9) liquid food made by boiling meat and/or vegetables in water
(10) do sth. very badly
(11) put a dead body in the ground

Exercise 8

➤ Using a Monolingual Dictionary (SB, p. 234)

Finding Out More about Words

➤ Text 4A, SB, p. 31

Answer the following questions that learners of English might typically ask. A monolingual dictionary will help you.

1 In Text 4A it says 'My family doesn't talk much' (l. 25), but I think I've heard people say 'My family don't ...'. Can you say both, or did I not listen properly?

____

2 What's the pronunciation of 'anonymous' (l. 13)? Which syllable is stressed? And how do you pronounce 'doughnut' (l. 31), like 'tough' and 'nut'?

____

3 In the text they spell the name of the colour 'gray' (l. 81). I thought it was 'grey'. Are both correct? Is there any difference in usage between them?

____

4 What do you say for 'eine Familie gründen'?

____

5 Do people say 'to raise a family' or 'to bring up a family'? If you can say both, what's the difference in meaning?

____

6 I've seen different words for 'grandfather' – grandad, granddad, granddaddy and grandpa. What's the difference, and how are they different from 'grandfather'?

____

Exercise 9

➤ Prepositions (*Cornelsen English Grammar*, §§ 246–250)

Prepositions

➤ Watch Your Language, SB, p. 35

Underline or circle the correct prepositions. Sometimes more than one is correct.

In our house, we always have turkey **at • on • to** Christmas. Mum starts to defrost it **at • on • over** Christmas Eve so that it's thawed out **by • till • until** Christmas Day. After we've opened our presents **at • on • to** the 25th, things start to hot up. Everybody lends a hand except Annie and Gary, who are only three and five, so they watch cartoon films **at • in • on** TV. I peel the spuds, Dad's our specialist **in • for • on** making the stuffing. My sister Jane does the Brussels sprouts and carrots. She's not keen **about • at • on** doing it, but she prefers it **instead of • over • to** peeling the potatoes. Then the phone rings. It's grandma. She always insists **at • in • on** phoning Mum to give her detailed instructions **about • concerning • on** how to cook the Christmas pudding, so Mum's **at • in • on** the phone with her for the next half hour. It takes so long because they both argue for ages **about • on • over** how to cook it.

Culture in Context

➤ Text 1, Context Box, SB, pp. 38–39

Exercise 1

a Collect examples of how the word *culture* is used on pp. 38 and 39 of the SB, noting whether it is used with or without the definite article. Write the examples down in their context, using the boxes below.

no article + *culture*	line	the + *culture*	line

b Explain why the definite article is sometimes used and why it is sometimes left out. A grammar book will help you.

➤ The Definite Article (*Cornelsen English Grammar*, §§ 182–188)

____

____

Talking in the Abstract

➤ Text 1, SB, p. 38

Exercise 2

Complete the sentences below by adding the definite article where necessary.

1 The emergence of youth culture is partly the result of the explosion of ________ consumer culture in the post-war period.

2 Rock 'n' roll was an important element of ________ American popular culture.

3 By the late 1970s and early 1980s, there were noticeable changes in ________ culture of young people in Britain.

4 Compared with the 1950s and 1960s, there was a decline in ________ youth culture based on gangs.

5 Environmentalists are worried about how the expansion of consumer culture worldwide will affect ________ nature.

6 She's writing a book on ________ history of climate change.

7 Psychologists are becoming increasingly interested in the effects of leisure on ________ modern society.

8 Our history teacher seems fascinated by ________ everyday life in the Middle Ages.

9 I disagree with the ideas on ________ utopian society which he described in his book.

10 Thomas Hobbes once described ________ human life as poor, nasty, brutish and short.

Exercise 3

Mind Mapping the Young

➤ Text 1, SB, p. 38

➤ Mind Mapping (SB, p. 222)

a Arrange the following terms in the mind map which has been started below. You may want to use some words more than once.

teen • youngster • adolescence • child • young people • adolescent • teenager • young people • youth • teenage • childhood

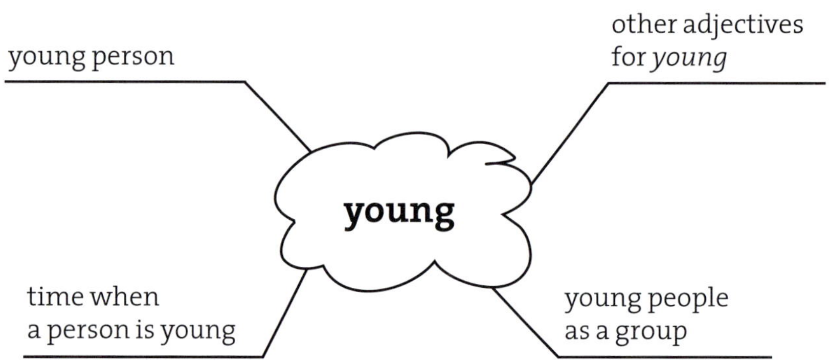

➤ Using a Monolingual Dictionary (SB, p. 234)

b Did you notice that the word *youth* has three different meanings? Explain the different meanings, using a monolingual dictionary to help you if necessary.

____

____

____

____

____

Idioms in Images

➤ Texts 1 and 2, Context Box, SB, pp. 38–40

Exercise 4

What idioms do the pictures below illustrate? Clue: they are taken from the SB. Explain briefly what the idioms mean.

1

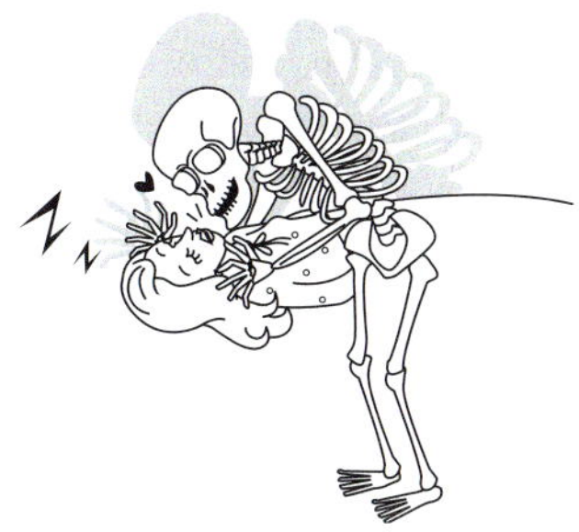

Idiom: ______________________

Meaning: ______________________

____

2

Idiom: ______________________

Meaning: ______________________

____

3

Idiom: ______________________

Meaning: ______________________

____

4

Idiom: ______________________

Meaning: ______________________

____

Worrying about Weight

➤ Text 3A, Getting Along in English, SB, pp. 42, 46

Exercise 5

Write an e-mail to a friend in an English-speaking country who is worried about being overweight. Look at Text 3A for useful vocabulary and ideas.

Helpline

➤ Text 4B, SB, p. 45

Exercise 6

You have got a holiday job in Britain working for a telephone helpline which specializes in teenage problems. Say what advice you would give to the following caller. You will probably find Text 4B useful.

'Hello, my name's Carol Singer. I've got a problem with my boyfriend. Whenever we go to a party he gets very drunk and starts acting really stupid. He's usually sick, which doesn't make him very popular, and I often have to get friends to help me carry him to the car. What would you advise me to do?'

Exercise 7

➤ Reading Narrative Prose (SB, p. 238); Glossary: Narrator and Point of View (SB, p. 258), Character and Characterization (p. 260), Action and Plot (p. 261)

Analysing a Story

➤ Text 5, SB, p. 47

Use the checklist below to analyse the short story 'Y2K.CHATRM43'.

1 What kind of *narrator* does the story use? Give examples.

2 Which parts of the story use *scenic presentation*, showing events as they occur, e.g. by using dialogues, describing a scene, depicting thoughts (e.g. by *interior monologues*)? Which parts of the story use *panoramic presentation*, i.e. events which happened over a period and are summarized in a few sentences?

3 Which characters in the story are *round* and complex, which are *flat* and simple?

4 Does the story mainly use *direct (explicit)* or *indirect (implicit) characterization*? Give examples from the text.

5 The diagram below shows the stages of the *plot*. Give a brief summary of the action in each stage and the line references.

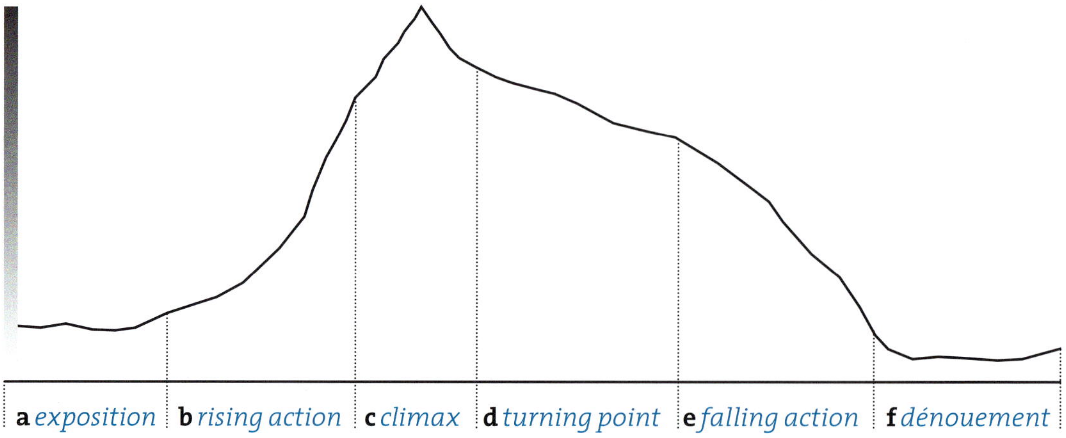

a ______________________________

b ______________________________

c ______________________________

d ______________________________

e ______________________________

f ______________________________

6 Find examples of *flashback* and *foreshadowing (anticipation)*.

____

____

____

Matching Phrases

Exercise 8

a Match the phrases on the left with those on the right so that the sentences make sense. The first one has been done for you. The prepositions will give you a clue.

Let's talk a bit more	in wasting time.
We should keep an eye	for UNICEF this year.
I'm not very good	about our chances of making a profit.
The firm is sceptical	on that man – he looks suspicious.
We need to raise more money	of the damage he's caused.
The boss doesn't believe	about global warming.
I've spent a lot of money	on my wife's hairstyle – it was so rude!
She hasn't had much experience	at telling lies.
I don't think he's aware	about your exam results.
I didn't like his comment	on repairing this car.
We urgently need to do something	with using a computer.

b Now choose five phrases and put them in sentences of your own.

Exercise 9

Breaking Records

a Form sentences from the facts given in note form on the left, using the superlative form of the adjective in each case, and by choosing the correct alternative from the three possibilities given on the right. (If you do not know an answer, make an intelligent guess!) The correct answers are given in the key. For an added challenge, give yourself a point for each correct answer and compare your results in class.

Example:

long road (world) ...
a) Route 66 (USA)
b) the Transamazonica (Brazil)
c) the Pan-American Highway

⚠ **Trouble spot**
It is wrong to say 'of the world' in this context in English.

The longest road in the world is the Pan-American Highway.

1 rare disease (world) ...
a) CJD (Creutzfeld Jacob disease)
b) smallpox
c) Marburg fever (Green Monkey disease)

2 busy port (Britain) ...
a) London
b) Liverpool
c) Dover

3 frequent cause of sudden death (the developed countries) ...
a) a stroke
b) AIDS
c) heart disease

4 bloody battle (history) ...
a) the Somme (1916)
b) Stalingrad (1942–1943)
c) Gettysburg (1863)

5 ... extensive underground railway (Europe), with a total length of 408 km
a) Moscow
b) Berlin
c) London

6 narrow street (the EU) ..., at one point being only 38 cm wide

a) Elgin Street in Bacup (UK)
b) Trianglen in Store Heddinge (Denmark)
c) Vicolo della Virilità (Italy)

7 large railway station (Britain) ...

a) Waterloo Station (London)
b) Waverley Station (Edinburgh)
c) Victoria Station (London)

8 complex motorway interchange (the UK) ..., with 18 routes at six levels

a) the M61–62 at Spaghetti Junction at Worsley (near Manchester)
b) the M6 at Spaghetti Junction at Gravelly Hill (near Birmingham)
c) the M3–M25 at Virginia Water (near London)

9 big and famous department store (London) ..., with a total selling floor space of 10.5 hectares

a) Selfridge's
b) Marks & Spencers
c) Harrods

10 heavy man (the USA), Jon Minnoch, was ... when he died in 1983

a) 215 kg
b) 362 kg
c) 442 kg

b Now make up your own quiz questions and play 'Who wants to be a millionaire?'.

Exercise 1

Famous Scientists

➤ Lead-in, SB, p. 54

a Link the scientific fields on the left and the famous scientists shown on the right. One matching pair has been done for you.

- **a** astronomy
- **b** biology
- **c** botany
- **d** chemistry
- **e** cartography
- **f** mathematics
- **g** physics
- **h** meteorology **1**
- **i** zoology

1 Alfred Wegener

2 Marie Curie

3 Gerardus Mercator

4 Charles Darwin

5 Carl von Linné

6 Louis Pasteur

7 Galileo Galilei

8 Alexander Fleming

9 Carl Friedrich Gauss

b Now find out what kinds of scientists they were and write a short sketch of their origins and achievements (e.g. two sentences).

Example:
Alfred Wegener (1880–1930) was a German meteorologist, geophysicist and explorer who was born in Berlin. He is best known for his theory of continental drift, i.e. the gradual movement of the continents over millennia.

Sharing Information ➤ Text 1B, SB, p. 58

Exercise 2

It is 2040. Your house is full of smart appliances. Imagine your fridge and your TV set are having a conversation on the Internet. How could they continue? Write about 100 words. The words and phrases below may help you.

appreciate sb./sth. • frustrating • give sb. an ultimatum • a human (being) • ignore sb./sth. • programme sth. (an appliance) • switch sth. on • teach sb. a lesson

The conversation begins like this:
Fridge: Hi, how are things?
TV: Not so good. John's messed up my programming again. He's thick! It's so simple, and all his kids can cope with it. Sometimes he just gives up and presses buttons at random, and that causes chaos with my programming.
F: I know the feeling. I've got a very sophisticated programme which tells humans when I'm out of milk, or eggs, or butter, but John ...

The Emperor's Thoughts ➤ Text 2A, SB, p. 60

Exercise 3

Choose **a** or **b**:

a Look at these scenes from 'The Flying Machine' and speculate on what the emperor is thinking when he learns about the man flying (cf. SB, ll. 14–44). Write down his thoughts.

1

2

3

4

5

6

7

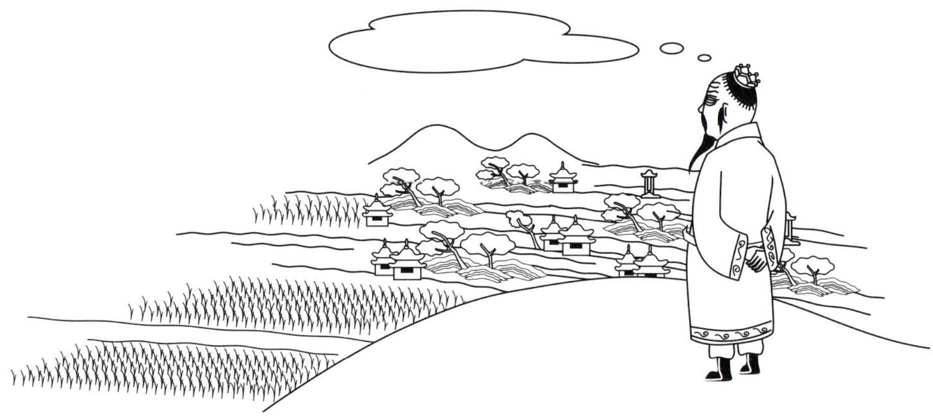

➤ Glossary: Interior Monologue (SB, p. 259, cf. Mode of Presentation)

b Write an interior monologue revealing the Emperor's thoughts when he hears about the man flying and then sees it with his own eyes (cf. SB, ll. 14–44).

Exercise 4

➤ Glossary: Imagery (SB, p. 268)

Images

a Join up the phrases in columns 1 and 2 to make suitable similes.

1	2
He ran like	dew.
Her fair hair shone in the sunlight like	a tiger.
She was purring with satisfaction, as	a rabbit looks at a snake.
He fought like	a panther ready to spring.
This meat's tough – it's like	gold.
The sports car stood with its engine revving, like	an antelope.
The rain falling on their faces was soft, like	an old boot.
He looked at her, hypnotized, as	a cat does when stroked.

b Combine the phrases in A and B to form metaphors. One has been done for you.

A	B
He has a heart of	hate.
She was	a sharp knife which left deep wounds.
Life is	Life contains many secrets.
You need nerves of	steel to survive such an experience.
His face was a mask of	a sickness full of pain.
The book of	the rock on which his life was built.
Her tongue was	stone.
Love is	a pudding full of plums.

c Now make up four sentences, using two similes and two metaphors of your own.

Technical Translating

➤ Text 3, SB, p. 67

Exercise 5

Translate the sentences below, which are taken from Text 3, into natural and accurate German. Take care with translating participle constructions.

1 'Hydrogen, pumped to the cell's negatively charged side (-), divides into protons and electrons.'

Wasserstoff, der in die negativ (-) geladene Seite der Zelle hineingepumpt wird, zerteilt sich in Protonen und Elektronen.

2 'A platinum membrane blocks electrons from moving directly to the positive side, forcing them through an external circuit as usable current.'

3 'Unlike a battery, a fuel cell generates current rather than simply storing it.'

4 'Zapping H2O with high-voltage electricity to break off the H is not cheap.'

5 'Fuel Cell generates electric current by combining hydrogen and oxygen, emitting only water from the tailpipe.'

6 'Besides powering cars and buses, fuel cells are used to provide power for orbiting spacecraft.'

Exercise 6 A Controlled Human Is a Safe Human

➤ Text 3, SB, p. 66

Look at task 4a (SB, p. 67) again. Write a short report about a future world where people can be controlled like rats, e.g. by the government or by big companies. They are being controlled for their own good, of course ... Tell the story from the point of view of a time traveller from the 21st century. Write about 200 words. You may find the following words and phrases from the SB useful:

signal • central computer • control sb./sth. • send a stimulus • cause sb. to do sth. • feel pleasure • safe lives • vast company • control over sth. • independent thoughts • nightmare • world

The report has been started for you:

When I stepped out of my time machine in the 22nd century, I was surprised to see that everybody was wearing little backpacks. I soon discovered why. I noticed that you never see people being run over by cars here ...

Talking about Statistics

Exercise 7

➤ Working with Numbers (SB, p. 226)

a Using the graph below, describe the general trends in British government spending on research and development (R&D) between 1986 and 2002. Write at least four sentences, using the phrases in the box.

the graph shows / indicates / deals with ... • compared with/to ... • to increase [- '-] / go up / rise from ... to ... between 1986 and 2002 ... • to decrease [- '-]/fall/drop/decline from ... to ... • an increase ['- -]/rise in R&D spending over five years ... • a decrease ['- -]/fall/drop/decline in expenditure of £1 bn ... • to increase/... by £0.5 bn = an increase/... of £0.5 bn ... • a sharp/rapid/steep increase/decrease • a gradual/slow increase/decrease ... • stay virtually the same / remain (fairly) constant ...

You should comment on:
1) total spending (including spending on the National Health Service [NHS])
2) defence spending
3) contributions to European Union R&D
4) expenditure on science and engineering

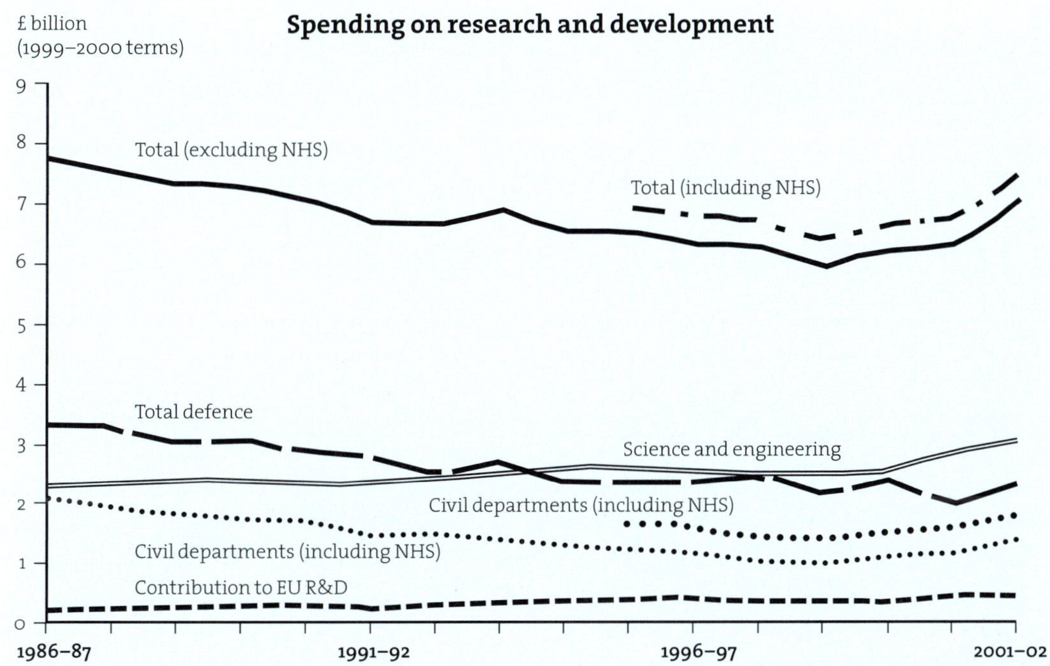

(Source: Office for National Statistics)

b Compare the two pie charts below. Comment on the role of business enterprise, the government and higher education in spending on R&D in the UK in 1999. Write at least four sentences. The words and phrases here may be helpful.

> the lion's share / the bulk of funds was provided by ... • X had the second largest/ biggest share of ... • Y accounted for / made up only 1 per cent of funding used for R&D ... whereas/while A was an important source of ..., accounting for 14% of ..., it ... • R&D work carried out / completed ... • it amounted to about/roughly/approximately 20% of the total ... • viz. • i.e.

Sector providing the funds

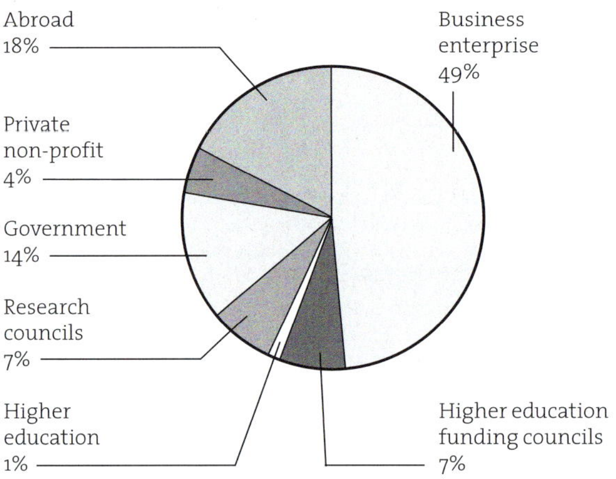

Sector carrying out the work

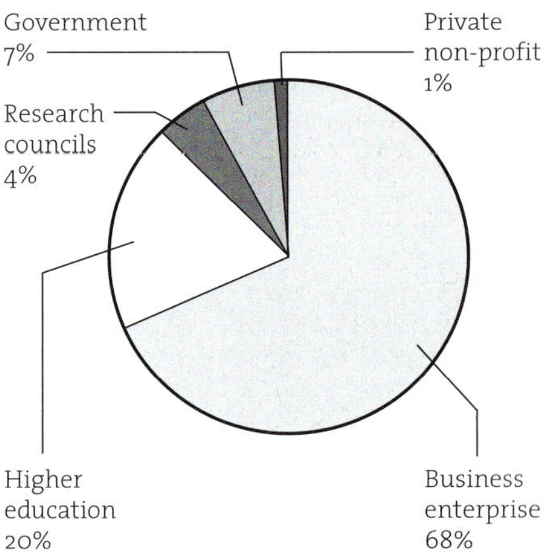

(Source: Office for National Statistics)

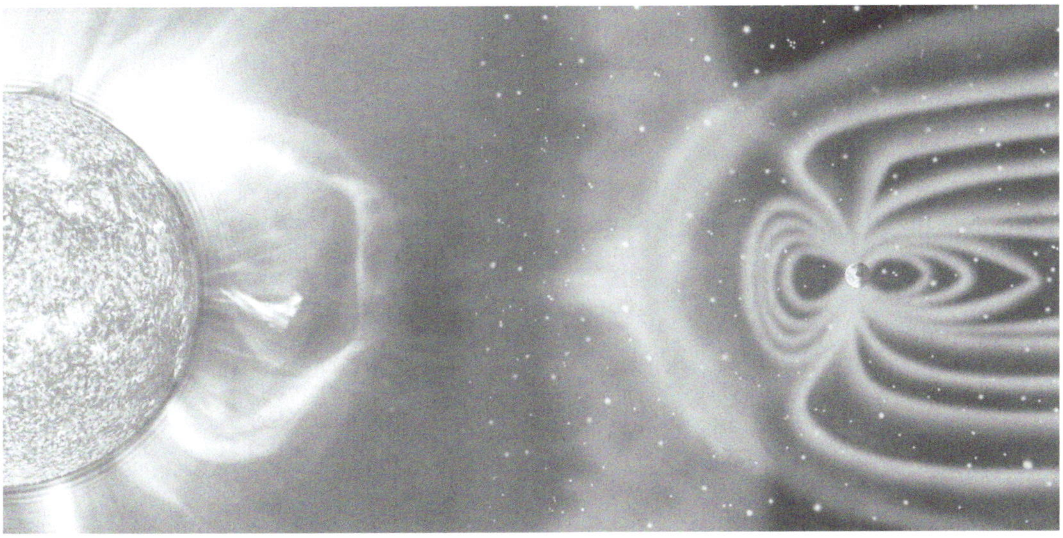

Protective Shield in Space

➤ Watch Your Language, SB, p. 73

Exercise 8

➤ Indirect Speech (*Cornelsen English Grammar*, §§ 151–163)

a Improve the style of the text below by using participles. The text has been divided into sections. You only need to write out the parts you have changed. The first section has been done for you.

A shower of particles from space millions of years ago may have led to drastic changes in the Earth's climate. This was followed by the extinction of life on a massive scale, which also killed off the dinosaurs.

... drastic changes in the Earth's climate, followed by ...

The solar wind, which is what experts call the electrically charged particles which are emitted by the sun, normally acts as a shield against showers of cosmic particles, which prevents too many energy-rich particles from raining down on our atmosphere.

Before they suddenly became extinct 65 million years ago, dinosaurs were the undisputed masters of the planet. 'Perhaps the Earth became too damp and cold for dinosaurs at that time,' Professor Fahr suggests. The reason for the sudden change in climate could have been excessive pressure on our cosmic umbrella.

The solar system does not stand still. It orbits the centre of the Milky Way once every 250 million years.

In the process it also passes through dense clouds of interstellar matter, which causes problems for the solar wind and thus for the Earth.

Although the solar wind normally protects the Earth from a hail of interstellar particles like a huge bullet-proof vest, this then suddenly changes, and up to a hundred times more particles rain down into the Earth's atmosphere.

There they smash the air molecules into fragments which are electrically charged. These function as condensation nuclei on which droplets of water form.

The result is 'dense cloud cover with more rain and snow and sinking temperatures,' says Professor Fahr, who bases his remarks on research worldwide.

b What examples of similes and metaphors can you find in the text?

Word Fields

➤ Texts 1A–B, SB, pp. 76–77

Exercise 1

a Words in two languages often cover different fields of meaning. Sometimes these differences can be shown in a diagram. Fill in the English equivalents to the German words below. The first one has been done for you.

larger ↑ smaller

English	German
forest	*Wald*
wood	

English	German
	Berg

English	German
	Stadt
	Dorf

English	German
	Strom
	Fluss
	Bach

b Now find out the main equivalents to the words *See*, *Ufer*, *Insel* and *Landschaft*. Use a bilingual and, if necessary, a monolingual dictionary. You do not need to put them in a diagram.

____

____

____

____

c Complete the sentences using the words dealt with above. Each word is used only once.

1 Most of Kent was covered by a huge ____________ in Saxon times, but since then a lot of the trees have been cut down.

2 The ____________ of Leipzig has always been an important publishing centre – the Leipzig Book Fair is very famous.

3 A little ____________ runs through our garden. It's so small that even our four-year-old son can jump across it.

4 Mittweida is a ____________ in Saxony with about 18,000 inhabitants.

5 Rome is built on seven ____________ . From the top of them, to the east you can see the Apennine ____________ , which rise to over 2000 metres.

6 There were several people sitting and fishing on the ____________ of the river.

7 The British ____________ are a group of ____________ in the Atlantic, off the coast of continental Europe.

8 Coleridge loved the dramatic ____________ of the Lake District. It was different from the ____________ he was used to in the South of England.

Exercise 2

A Bargain Planet! ➤ Lead-in, SB, p. 74

Look at the following ad, which has been placed in the *Galactic Guardian*. Create a dialogue between Gabriel Angelino, estate agent for Celestial Real Estate Inc., and a potential customer. Gabriel is very concerned that the planet should be bought by a responsible client, because the previous owners, Adam and Eve and their descendants, did not look after it properly. Gabriel mentions the problems he had with them. You may wish to use some of the vocabulary given below. Write about 200 words.

PLANET FOR SALE

Earth: One previous owner. Seven spacious continents, three climate zones with North and South poles attached, solar-powered central heating, with own moon. Convenient for Milky Way. Good views of outer galaxy. Some renovation work necessary due to ecological neglect by previous owner. Reasonably priced. Suitable for first-time buyer. Apply to *Celestial Real Estate Inc.* (not Sundays).

plenty of sth. • have something to suit all tastes • come supplied with sth. • sun: only 93 million miles away • bargain • 3 billion galactic crowns • how come ...? • use sth. up • natural resource(s) • terrible waste of sth. • repeat our/a/... mistake • make a serious/higher/better/ ... offer

Exercise 3

Barbara's Secret ➤ Texts 1A–B, SB, pp. 76–77

Barbara keeps a secret diary in English. She is very poetic, but grammar is not her strong point. Find and correct the 15 grammar mistakes she has made in the text below.

The most of my friends spend a lot of their time hearing CDs or looking television, but I would rather go for long walks in the countryside. Sometimes I just stand there and hear the birds. Birdsong makes me feel calmly. What's more, I can tell from their song which sort of bird they are. I get very excited when I hear a new bird for the first time. They sound so beautifully in the clear morning air. Whenever I have the chance, I also enjoy to walk slow across a lawn when the grass has just been mown and is smelling so freshly. My friends don't take me serious. When I tell them what I feel about the nature, they look at me strange as if to say that on the surface I seem so normally, but that I've often got such strange ideas. I've not dared to tell them yet that what I like most is to put my feet in the village pond and feel the fish nibbling gentle at my toes. But we all have our little secrets, don't we?

Analysing a Poem

➤ Text 1B, SB, p. 77

Exercise 4

➤ Reading Poetry (SB, p. 241), Glossary: Poetry (SB, p. 256)

Use the guidelines below to analyse the poem 'The Lake Isle of Innisfree'. Answer each question with one or two sentences.

General

1 Is the poem a) *narrative* (i.e. telling a story), b) *descriptive* or c) other?

2 What event or situation is presented in the poem?

3 What is the poem's theme or topic?

4 Who is the speaker and who is he or she talking to?

5 What is the poem's intention?

Structure

6 How many *stanzas* are there?

7 What is the *rhythm* and *rhyme scheme*?

Language

8 Is the language *simple* or *elevated*, i.e. 'poetic'? Give examples.

9 What *repetitions* and *contrasts* are there? What effect do they have?

10 What *imagery* does the poem contain, e.g. similes, metaphors,symbols?

Exercise 5

➤ Glossary: News Story (SB, p. 262)

A News Story

➤ Text 2, SB, p. 80

Write a short newspaper report for a local paper about the ice storm described in Text 2. Supply a headline (cf. the examples on pp. 112–113 of the SB) and try to make the report as realistic as possible. If you need extra help, you could look at newspaper articles in English (especially reports of bad weather) on the Internet. Remember that a news story will probably not deal with the same things as the short story. Write about 200 words. You may like to use the following words and phrases, some of which are from Text 2.

freezing rain • slippery • skating rink • power lines • collapse • plunge sb./sth. into darkness • bring sth. to a standstill • restore power • livestock • eyes freeze shut • take pity on sb./sth.

Exercise 6

Recycling Words

➤ Context Box, Text 3A, SB, pp. 82–83

Complete the following sentences by recycling words and phrases from the Context Box and from Text 3A.

If we wish to survive on Planet Earth, we need to develop ________________ (1). Only by giving back to the land as much as we take from it can we stop the destruction of the Earth's natural ________________ (2). There is no doubt that some progress is being made – in many countries there has been an increase in people's environmental ________________ (3). This is reflected in the numbers of people who ________________ (4). By doing this, they are helping industry to re-use products and avoid waste. This also means that we do not need to bury so much rubbish in ________________ (5). As a result of this change in attitudes to the environment, the public has been more prepared to listen to environmental groups, as well as to individual ________________ (6). Industry, too, has played its part. For example, compared with the past, cars nowadays ________________ (7). Similarly, there has been a drastic reduction in many ________________ (8). However, there is still a long way to go in improving air quality. Climate change is still continuing, partly caused by the destruction of tropical rainforests, which provide a large part of the world's ________________ (9). Cutting down trees leads to a rise in the amount of carbon dioxide in the atmosphere, and this in turn results in ________________ (10). Another problem is the effect of emissions on the upper atmosphere, leading to ________________ (11). In order to prevent ecological catastrophe we need to put more pressure on governments so that they pass ________________ (12).

Useful Words

➤ Watch Your Language, SB, p. 89

Exercise 7

➤ The *To*-infinitive, The Gerund (*Cornelsen English Grammar*, §§ 122–123, 136–143)

The following sentences are taken from a speech by an environmental activist. Place the verbs in brackets in either the *to*-infinitive or the gerund. Check in a dictionary or a grammar book if you are not sure which construction to use.

1 If we keep ________________ (use up) the planet's resources at the present rate, they will soon be exhausted.

2 We need to stop ________________ (pollute) the Earth – it's the only planet we've got.

3 The rich nations, especially the US, must try much harder ________________ (set) a good example to the rest of the world in their treatment of the environment.

4 We should avoid ________________ (use) fossil fuels where there are cleaner alternatives such as wind and solar power.

5 We must learn ________________ (treat) nature with much more respect instead of ________________ (regard) it simply as a source of raw materials.

6 Environmental organizations can teach the public ________________ (become) more environmentally aware.

7 If we are serious about ________________ (slow down) global warming, we must not delay ________________ (introduce) a carbon tax.

8 Companies are often reluctant ________________ (conserve) resources because they are afraid it will reduce their profits.

9 Where necessary, governments must force industry ________________ (be) more environment-friendly.

10 Changing our attitudes to the environment also involves ________________ (rethink) our whole approach to consumerism.

'It's his contribution to the environment.'

Exercise 8

➤ Giving a Talk or Presentation (SB, p. 254)

Recruiting More Eco-warriors

➤ Texts 3A–C, SB, pp. 83–86

Give a short talk of three minutes on one aspect of the environment. The list below gives you some ideas for a topic. Whatever topic you choose, try to persuade your audience that they need to do more for the environment. Use the guidelines in the SB to prepare your talk. You may find some of the phrases used in Exercises 6 and 7 useful.

- Global warming
- Endangered species
- The threat to the ozone layer
- The Gulf Stream
- World without water
- Who needs rainforests?
- Industry – the enemy of the environment?

As an audience member, use the checklist below to assess how good the other talks were. Discuss your results in class. Take care with your criticisms and try to formulate them constructively.

Talk assessment checklist	yes	no
1 Was the talk easy to understand?	■	■
2 Did the speaker speak clearly and at the right speed?	■	■
3 Did the speaker use handouts and/or visual material?	■	■
4 If OHP transparencies were used, were they clear and could they be easily read by people in the back row?	■	■
5 Did the speaker stand straight, facing the audience, and did he or she keep eye contact?	■	■
6 Did the speaker begin with a lively, interesting introduction?	■	■
7 Were the main points of the talk expressed clearly?	■	■
8 Were enough specific examples given to illustrate important points?	■	■
9 Did the speaker summarize the main points at the end of the talk?	■	■
10 Did the speaker go over time, i.e. take longer than three minutes?	■	■

11 How could the speaker have improved the talk? ______________________

____

____

____

____

____

____

Where Am I?

Exercise 9

Seeing is one of the most important senses, and the other senses are often neglected. Help yourself to become aware of the other senses by preparing a description of a place which you and your classmates are likely to know. Close your eyes and imagine you are there now. Describe what your other senses register and let the rest of the class guess where you are.

Example:
I am lying outside in the fresh air. The ground feels soft. The air feels warm, though there is a breeze. The people around me sound happy. Some of them don't make any sound at all. The air smells and tastes salty. There is a distant sound.

Alternatively, you can describe a situation like this:
I can hear other young people shouting and running about, and the sound of a ball.
I can feel the vibrations of feet on the floor.
I can smell people's sweat.

Make up some examples of your own using the different forms, e.g. *I can hear* ... or *It sounds* ....

Spot the Wrong Prepositions

➤ Sections 1–3, SB, pp. 76–78, 80–81, 83–86

Exercise 10

➤ Prepositions (*Cornelsen English Grammar*, §§ 246–250)

In the following sentences 12 prepositions are incorrect. Cross out the wrong ones and replace them with the correct ones.

1 At Earth Day we all used to sing on the environment.

2 Over the past twenty years there has been a big reduction of the use of leaded petrol, because many people are worried about its effects on children's health.

3 There is a saying that a cynic knows the price for everything and the value on nothing.

4 There was ice at the windows. It reminded me on the winters of my childhood.

5 The government is determined to introduce a tax on pollution.

6 In average, you can save 10% on heating costs if you turn the heating down by 1°C.

7 There has been a rise of the Earth's temperature over the last few decades.

8 The original Garden of Eden was a symbol for paradise.

9 Many people are far too sentimental over animals and nature.

10 When we consume things we do not really need, we are doing this on the expense of the environment.

Exercise 1 Players in the World Economy

➤ Lead-in, SB, p. 90

Fill as many of the blanks in the texts as you can without looking in the SB. Then check the vocabulary boxes in the SB, pp. 90–91, and fill the remaining blanks.

As a ____________ I buy and sell shares on the ____________ ____________ for other people. I need to keep myself informed about the latest ____________ trends, e.g. whether we're approaching a ____________ which would lead to a drop in share values. I also need to know the latest ____________ of the major world ____________ – the dollar, the euro, the yen and the pound.

I'm a ____________. Crops like cocoa are an important element in ____________ of ____________ countries like Ghana. My country is heavily ____________, so it has to ____________ as much of its ____________ materials to the industrialized world as possible. Foreign multinationals like to invest in Ghana because of the cheap ____________. Most of us workers live in ____________. We know that we are being ____________, but what can we do?

I'm just an ordinary ____________ who buys goods in the shops. Of course, if people like me didn't ____________ the products of industry, the ____________ would collapse. I have to be careful when I ____________ money. Like everybody else, I'm ____________ by TV ____________. The big companies try to ____________ a ____________ for things we don't really need, but I'm a single parent, so I have to economize.

I was an ____________ in a car ____________ in Michigan, but I became ____________ when my company decided to ____________ its ____________ ____________ radically by firing all its workers. It claimed its factory was ____________ because the US economy was in ____________. It moved its ____________ abroad. Since then I've been living on ____________. I also try to ____________ my family by doing odd jobs for the neighbours.

Fighting for Your Rights

➤ Text 1, SB, p. 92

Exercise 2

Time has moved on since Willy Loman's days (cf. Text 1). Ben Loman, his grandson, who is also a salesman, is unhappy with the way his boss treats him. He has asked his trade union representative, Paul Casey, to put his case to Ben's boss. Fill in the gaps to fit the context. Begin by reading through the whole dialogue so that all your answers make sense.

Boss: Good morning, Mr Casey. What can I do for you?

Casey: It's about ______________________________ .

B: Oh yes, he's a problem. He wants an office job, but I don't have one vacant.

C: But surely you ______________________________

______________________________ .

B: Believe me, Mr Casey, I'd like to do something for him. I appreciate that he's been working for us for over 30 years, but I just don't have any office jobs vacant at the moment.

C: Perhaps ______________________________ your Boston branch?

B: No, I can't send him to work there. The truth is, I don't want him to represent our company at all. He's old. He's past it.

C: He told me ______________________________ in commissions.

B: Yes, he did, but that was 20 years ago, for God's sake!

C: Maybe, but you can't expect a man in his fifties to work as well as a young man like yourself. You have a responsibility to your older employees. As his grandfather said to me once, 'You can't treat a man like an orange – eat ______________________________

______________________________ .

B: Orange or no orange, I have a business to run. I can't be sentimental about an old man. It's a tough world out there.

C: Well then, if you won't ______________________________

____

______________________________ .

B: Responsibility? What about my responsibility to my shareholders? And who are these colleagues who support him? As for the strike meeting this afternoon, you must be crazy. Do you realize how much a strike would cost us?

Exercise 3

➤ Using a Monolingual Dictionary (SB, p. 234)

Foreigner Talk

Axel Schmidt is working at a firm in Britain. His English is quite good, but he keeps making mistakes which lead to misunderstandings with his British friends. Find the mistake in each of the following, explain the misunderstanding and say what the correct version should be. In some cases you will probably need the help of a good monolingual dictionary.

1 'My chief says I have to work overtime.'
'Your chief, Axel? What's the name of your tribe?'

2 'I like my work in the bureau very much.'
'Oh, it doesn't sound as though there's much room in there.'

3 'To help the developing countries, we must give them much more aids.'
'I would have thought they had enough problems already.'

4 'Axel, have you seen Angela Dawson anywhere?'
'Yes, I've just seen her on the floor.'
'What was she doing on the floor? Did she fall or something?'

5 'I have made many different works in the last ten years.'
'Gosh, Axel, I didn't know you were a writer.'

6 'Axel, can I talk to you for a few minutes about this Selfridges order?'
'Of course. Please, take place.'
'Couldn't I just have a seat?'

7 'Most of the employees in the firm seem to be very happy when they are on the job.'
'Really, Axel, you mustn't keep talking about sex all the time!'

Prepositions at Work

➤ Texts 2A–C, SB, pp. 95–98

Exercise 4

Circle or underline the correct prepositions from the alternatives given. In some cases more than one preposition is correct.

Donald MacNeil lives with his wife **at • in • on** a Glasgow housing estate. He hasn't had a job now **during • for • in** ten years. Although Donald, who used to work **at • by • in** a steelworks, has often searched **after • for • on** work, there is no longer much demand **after • for • in** steelworkers due to the decline **in • of • on** the steel industry. The family are dependent **from • of • on** state benefits. Apart from the rent, they spend most of their money **for • in • on** food. Most of the furniture is old, and their TV is **at • in • on** its last legs.

Collocations

Exercise 5

➤ Using a Monolingual Dictionary (SB, p. 234)

a Monolingual dictionaries give a lot of information on collocations, i.e. the words that normally go together with the word you have looked up. Study the entry 'business' from the *Oxford Advanced Learner's Dictionary*.

busi·ness /ˈbɪznəs/ *noun*
TRADE| **1** [U] the activity of making, buying, selling or supplying goods or services for money SYN COMMERCE, TRADE: *business contacts / affairs / interests* ◇ *a business investment* ◇ *It's been a pleasure to* ***do business with*** *you.* ◇ *She has set up* ***in business*** *as a hairdresser.* ◇ *When he left school, he* ***went into business*** *with his brother.* ◇ *She works in the computer business.*—see also AGRIBUSINESS, BIG BUSINESS, SHOW BUSINESS
WORK| **2** [U] work that is part of your job: *Is the trip to Rome* ***business or pleasure?*** ◇ *a business lunch* ◇ *He's away* ***on business.*** **3** [U] the amount of work done by a company, etc.; the rate or quality of this work: *Business was bad.* ◇ *Business was booming.* ◇ *Her job was to drum up* (= increase) *business.* ◇ *How's business?*
COMPANY| **4** [C] a commercial organization such as a company, shop/store or factory: *to have / start / run your own business* ◇ *business premises* ◇ *She works in the family business.* ◇ *They've got a small catering business.*
RESPONSIBILITY| **5** [U] something that concerns a particular person or organization: *It is the business of the police to protect the community.* ◇ *I shall* ***make it my business*** *to find out who is responsible.* ◇ *My private life is* ***none of your business*** (= does not concern you). ◇ *It's* ***no business of yours*** *who I invite to the party.*
IMPORTANT MATTERS| **6** [U] important matters that need to be dealt with or discussed: *the main business of the meeting* ◇ *He has some* ***unfinished business*** *to deal with.*
EVENT| **7** [sing.] (usually with an adjective) a matter, an event or a situation: *That plane crash was a terrible business.* ◇ *I found the whole business very depressing.* ◇ *The business of the missing tickets hasn't been sorted out.*
BEING A CUSTOMER| **8** [U] (*especially AmE*) = CUSTOM (3): *We're grateful for your business.*

IDM **any other ˈbusiness** the things that are discussed at the end of an official meeting that do not appear on the AGENDA: *I think we've finished item four. Now is there any other business?*—see also AOB **be in ˈbusiness** (*informal*) to have everything that you need in order to be able to start sth immediately: *All we need is a car and we'll be in business.* **be the ˈbusiness** (*spoken, slang*) to be very good **business as ˈusual** a way of saying that things will continue as normal in spite of a difficult situation **ˌbusiness is ˈbusiness** a way of saying that financial and commercial matters are the important things to consider and you should not be influenced by friendship, etc. **get down to ˈbusiness** to start dealing with the matter that needs to be dealt with, or doing the work that needs to be done: *Let's get down to business right away—we'll stop for coffee later.* **go about your ˈbusiness** to do the things that you normally do: *streets filled with people going about their daily business* **have no business doing sth | have no business to do sth** to have no right to do sth: *You have no business being here.* **like ˈnobody's business** (*BrE, spoken*) very much, very fast, very well, etc: *I've been working like nobody's business to get it finished in time.* **not be in the business of doing sth** not intending to do sth (which it would be surprising for you to do): *I'm not in the business of getting other people to do my work for me.* **out of ˈbusiness** having stopped operating as a business because there is no more money or work available: *The new regulations will* ***put*** *many small businesses* ***out of business.*** ◇ *Some travel companies will probably* ***go out of business*** *this summer.*—more at MEAN *v.*, MIND *v.*, PLY *v.*

(Entry from *Oxford Advanced Learner's Dictionary* [sixth edition])

b Connect the phrases in the two lists below to form the correct collocations. The first one has been done for you.

1 A strong euro will put	a into business with her father.
2 The firm had so many debts that it went	b down to business – we've not got much time.
3 Mr Jones is away	c business with your firm.
4 We need to get	d in business as investment consultants.
5 She's decided to go	e many firms out of business.
6 It's a pleasure to do	f out of business.
7 They've set up	g on urgent business, I'm afraid.

c Now write four sentences of your own using these collocations.

Exercise 6

➤ The Definite Article (*Cornelsen English Grammar*, § 183)

Nice Work

➤ Texts 2A, 4A–B, SB, pp. 95, 102–103

a Complete the text so that it shows the correct use or non-use of the definite article.

I like _____ work. It fascinates me so much that I could sit and look at _____ work for hours. To be honest, _____ work that I do in _____ office is boring, so I often play games on _____ computer. Sometimes I listen to _____ music when the boss isn't watching.

He's crazy. Like a lot of top executives in industry, he loves _____ power, especially _____ power he has over his workers. In fact, _____ life at _____ work would be awful if I didn't have _____ music to keep me happy. You'd think that _____ working at a firm in _____ computer games industry would be fascinating, but like _____ most jobs in _____ British industry nowadays, it's pretty tedious.

b Write sentences of your own, using the following words twice, once in a general sense without the definite article and once in a specific meaning with the article. You will find examples of their use in the texts in the SB (cf. above).

poverty • affluence • freedom • thrift • society

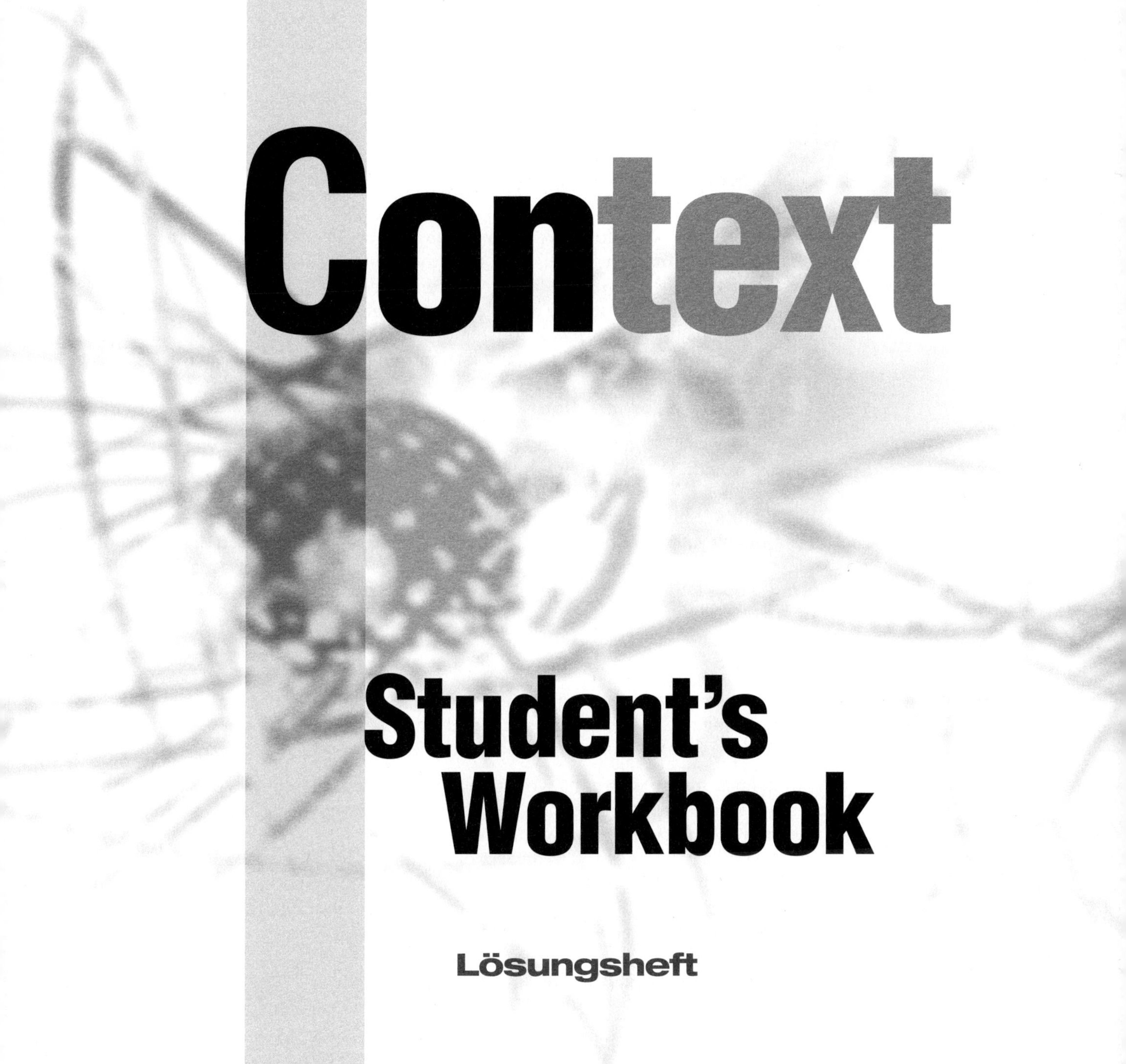

Context

Student's Workbook

Lösungsheft

Cornelsen

Chapter One

1 Describing a Picture

The main focus of the painting appears to be on the turkey in the centre of the picture.

The eye then moves to the older woman (probably the grandmother) holding the turkey, and her husband, both in the background of the painting.

Finally, we see the rest of the family at the table in the foreground – both the younger members, the grandchildren, and the older ones, who are probably the grandchildren's parents.

The perspective and the way the elements are arranged in the picture gives us the feeling that we are actually taking part in the meal as one of the guests or as part of the family.

2 Talking about the Past

Example:
When I was a boy, we didn't have much money. We could only afford sweets once a week. In those days not many people had TV, so in the evenings we listened to the radio, or played cards or other games together. We often used to go to the cinema on Saturdays. After school us kids used to play outside in the street – it wasn't as dangerous as now, with all the cars nowadays. It was much more fun than all these computer games, and much healthier. You didn't see so many fat children back then.

3 Overhearing a Conversation

... (that) she was having lots of problems with you. She said (that) you were so secretive that you wouldn't even tell her who you were going out with at night. And she said (that) you weren't very sensible and (she was afraid that) you'd got in with the wrong crowd. She said (that) she was worried that you might get pregnant. She said (that) you were so unreasonable and that she had tried to discuss it sensibly with you so that you could work out a solution together but you just wouldn't listen. And the other woman said (that) young people today were very rebellious and (that) parents needed to be strict – it was the only solution.

4 Describing Trends

a The number of people living on their own, i.e. without a family, increased slightly.
The percentage of married couples dropped by 3.5%.
The number of single-parent households rose between 1990 and 2000.

b In the past a man who got a woman pregnant was supposed to marry her, and often pressure would be put on the man to make sure this happened. It was regarded as bad for a woman to become pregnant without being married.
Because many marriages end in divorce or separation it is much more acceptable nowadays for people to remarry. People who remarry often have children from their first marriage. Stepparents and stepchildren are more common than they used to be. People also have a more relaxed attitude to marriage as a result.

5 Family Backgrounds

Example:
Born: 1879, in Gori, Georgia
Occupation: government head
Parents' occupations: father was a shoemaker, mother did odd jobs, e.g. washing clothes, baking bread, going on errands, sewing
Family situation: the family was very poor and was constantly in debt
Childhood experiences: this person, who did not get enough to eat, was often very badly beaten by the father
Other details: originally studied at a theological seminary to become a priest
(Answer: Joseph Stalin)

6 Family Types

Example:
Single-parent family
Mary Littlehampton is a single parent who lives alone in a small flat in Leicester with her 5-month-old son Gary. Her husband Derek left her two months ago. Derek did not want a child, but Mary was against having an abortion. Derek is now living with another woman and is planning to get a divorce. Because Gary is still very small, Mary cannot go out to work full time yet, but she has got a part-time job as an office cleaner. Her mother looks after Gary while Mary is at work. Mary does not have much money and finds it hard to pay the rent for the flat and the electricity and gas bills.

7 Is This What I Died for?

1 starving 2 frozen 3 thaw 4 guts 5 hatchet 6 saws 7 sink
8 detergent 9 soup 10 screwed up 11 buried

8 Finding Out More about Words

1 Both are possible with 'family' in both British and American English. Look up the pattern after collective nouns in general in a good grammar book.
2 The adjective 'anonymous' (l. 13) is pronounced [ə'nɒnɪməs ☆ ə'nɑːn-], with the stress on the second syllable. The noun 'doughnut' (l. 31) is pronounced ['dəʊnʌt ☆ 'doʊ-].
3 Both are correct, but 'gray' is only common in American English, while the normal British spelling is 'grey'.
4 The correct form is 'to start a family'.
5 People say both 'to raise a family' and 'to bring up a family'. There is no difference in meaning.
6 The word 'grandfather' is more formal, the others being informal:
'grandad' – both in British and American English
'granddad' – especially in American English
'granddaddy' – only in American English
'grandpa' – both in British and American English

9 Prepositions

at Christmas – on Christmas Eve – by Christmas Day – on the 25th – on TV – specialist in – keen on – prefers it to peeling – insists on phoning – instructions about/on – on the phone – argue for ages about/over

Chapter Two

1 Culture in Context

a

no article + culture	line	the + culture	line
youth culture	1	the 'youth culture'	10
post-war consumer culture	3	the American popular culture centred on rock 'n' roll	13
British post-war youth culture	12		
British culture	17	the youth culture of the time	CB

b *Cornelsen English Grammar*, § 183, on abstract nouns:
'A noun can be without the definite article when it is used in a very general sense.'
'... a noun has a definite article when it is made more concrete or when we specify which we mean, e.g. by means of an *of*-phrase [...] or a relative clause ...'
Notice that the example *the American popular culture centred on rock 'n' roll* is a participle phrase which has the same function as a relative clause (cf. § 153d).

2 Talking in the Abstract

1 ... of consumer culture ...
2 ... of American popular culture.
3 ... in the culture of young people in Britain.
4 ... in the youth culture based on gangs.
5 ... affect nature.
6 ... on the history of climate change.
7 ... on modern society.
8 ... by everyday life in the Middle Ages.
9 ... on the utopian society which he described in his book.
10 ... described human life as ...

3 Mind Mapping the Young

a

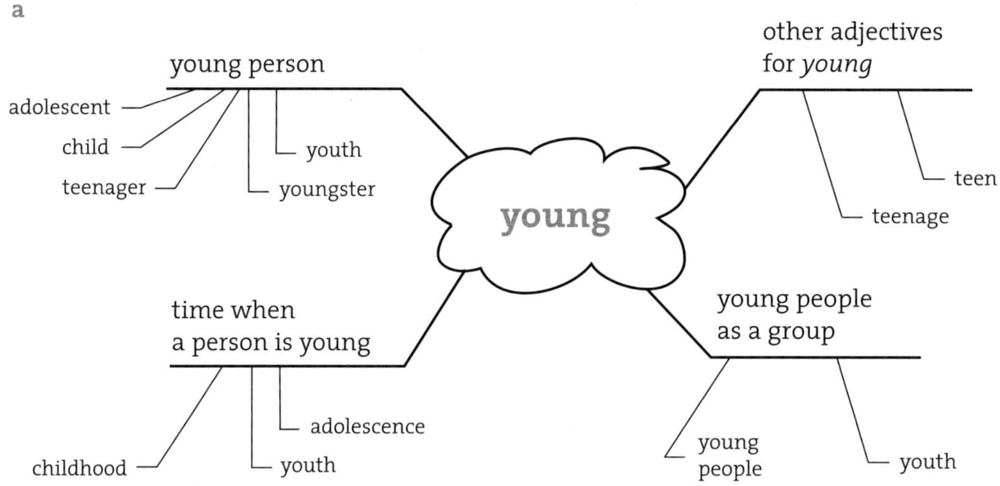

b 1) young man (countable noun: plural *youths*)
2) time when young (uncountable, usu. no article)
3) young people considered as a group (uncountable, also with article, followed by plural verb)

4 Idioms in Images

1 the kiss of death = sth. that seems good, but is certain to make sth. else fail
2 turn the spotlight on sb. = focus attention on sb.
3 over the moon = extremely happy or excited
4 go bananas = go crazy or become angry

5 Worrying about Weight

Example:

Hi Janet,

Thx for your mail. Why do you want to lose weight? You're not fat. And are you sure it's a good idea to skip breakfast and lunch? I don't think there's much point in dieting. You may lose some weight while you're on the diet, but when you stop dieting you'll probably put on weight again. That's what happened with me, at least. In the end I decided it wasn't worth it. Who cares if you've not got the figure of a model? How many women do? I've cut down on chocolate and started to eat more fruit and vegetables. I also play squash – it's much more fun than dieting. ;-)

ATB

Sandra

6 Helpline

Possible answer:
I would tell the caller that she could start by telling him how dangerous binge drinking is. It puts strain on your liver and can kill you if your blood glucose level falls very low. If he's very drunk and is sick, there's also a danger of him choking on his own vomit. That might even be fatal. She could also tell him how bad alcohol is for his fertility.
If he still won't listen, it's worth pointing out that prevention is better than cure. She should persuade him to have something to eat before going to a party. He could get some fish and chips or a hamburger. That would help to soak up some of the alcohol. She could tell him that he should never drink alcohol on an empty stomach. And if he still drinks too much at the party, she could get him to drink water. He shouldn't be left alone. If he's in a really bad way, she may need to take him to a hospital.

7 Analysing a Story

1 It uses a first-person narrator. For example, it says on l. 1: 'At the end of this story I'm supposed to turn off my computer ...'. And on ll. 5–6: 'As usual, I walked the last couple of blocks....'.
2 Scenic presentation is used on ll. 11–43, 108–154, 162–165 and 170–231 (all dialogues), and on ll. 87–105 (interior monologue). Panoramic presentation is used to describe the development of the chat room over time on ll. 44–86.
3 The main characters Adrien and Joel are round and complex, whereas the other less important characters are flat and simple.
4 The story mainly uses indirect (implicit) characterization, e.g. the developing relationship between Joel and Adrien on ll. 170–230. There are also some examples of direct (explicit) characterization, e.g. when Adrien calls Joel a 'gloomy Gus' on l. 18, and when Joel comments on Fred's character on ll. 95–96.
5 a exposition: ll. 1–10 (the computer theme is introduced, also the main characters)
b rising action: ll. 11–138 (conflict between Adrien and Joel, life in the chat room)
c climax: ll. 139–140 (Sonja's reaction will decide if the chat room stays open)
d turning point: ll 141–165 (serious discussion in chat room)
e falling action: ll. 166–205 (Sonja's identity revealed)
f dénouement: ll. 206–231 (Adrien and Joel's relationship develops, conflict resolved)
6 There are two examples of flashback, on ll. 5–43, looking back at the argument between Adrien and Joel, and on ll. 44–86, reviewing the history of the chat room. There is an example of foreshadowing (anticipation) at the beginning of the story on ll. 1–4, when Joel looks ahead to the time when he will finish the story and perhaps switch the computer off.

8 Matching Phrases

a We should keep an eye on that man – he looks suspicious.
I'm not very good at telling lies.
The firm is sceptical about our chances of making a profit.
We need to raise more money for UNICEF this year.
The boss doesn't believe in wasting time.
I've spent a lot of money on repairing this car.
She hasn't had much experience with using a computer.
I don't think he's aware of the damage he's caused.
I didn't like his comment on my wife's hairstyle – it was so rude!
We urgently need to do something about global warming.

b – –

9 Breaking Records

a

1 The rarest disease in the world is smallpox.
2 The busiest port in Britain is Dover.
3 The most frequent cause of sudden death in the developed countries is heart disease.
4 The bloodiest battle in history was the Somme in 1916.
5 London has the most extensive underground railway in Europe, with a total length of 408 km.
6 The narrowest street in the EU is the Vicolo della Virilità in Italy, at one point being only 38 cm wide.
7 The largest railway station in Britain is Waterloo Station in London.
8 The most complex motorway interchange in the UK is the M6 at Spaghetti Junction at Gravelly Hill near Birmingham, with 18 routes at six levels.
9 The biggest and most famous department store in London is Harrods, with a total selling floor space of 10.5 hectares.
10 The heaviest man in the USA, Jon Minnoch, was 442 kg when he died in 1983.

b --

Chapter Three

1 Famous Scientists

a

a	astronomy	**7**	Galileo Galilei
b	biology	**8**	Alexander Fleming
c	botany	**5**	Carl von Linné
d	chemistry	**6**	Louis Pasteur
e	cartography	**3**	Gerardus Mercator
f	mathematics	**9**	Carl Friedrich Gauss
g	physics	**2**	Marie Curie
h	meteorology	**1**	Alfred Wegener
i	zoology	**4**	Charles Darwin

b

Galileo Galilei (1564–1642) was an Italian astronomer and mathematician who was born in Pisa. He argued that the Earth moved round the sun, not vice versa, and came into conflict with the Catholic Church as a result of this view.

Alexander Fleming (1881–1955) was a Scottish biologist working in the field of bacteriology. In 1928 he discovered penicillin.

Carl von Linné (1707–1778), often known as Linnaeus in English, was the Swedish botanist who founded the modern system of botanical classification.

Louis Pasteur (1822–1895) was a French chemist and microbiologist. He proved that food, for example, went bad as a result of micro-organisms. Pasteurization is named after him. In pasteurization milk is heated at 63–66°C for 30 minutes or at 72°C for 15 seconds, which kills many of the bacteria in the milk.

Gerardus Mercator (1512–1594) was a geographer, cartographer and mathematician from Flanders in modern Belgium. Mercator's map projection is still one of the most widely used map projections even today, although it distorts the size of areas at the top and bottom of the map (e.g. Greenland looks as large as South America, although it is only 10% of the size of the latter).

Carl Friedrich Gauss (1777–1855) was a German mathematician, born in Brunswick (Braunschweig). He wrote the first modern book on number theory and was a pioneer in the use of mathematics in fields like gravitation, magnetism and electricity. His picture was on the 10-mark note before the mark was replaced by the euro in 2002.

Marie Curie, née *Sklodowska* (1867–1934), was a Polish physicist who emigrated to France in 1891. Together with her French husband, Pierre Curie (1859–1906), she worked on radioactivity and discovered radium. In 1903 she shared the Nobel Prize for Physics with her husband and Henri Becquerel (1852–1908). In 1911 she was also awarded the Nobel Prize for Chemistry.

Charles Darwin (1809–1882) was an English zoologist who made a scientific survey of the South Pacific on HMS Beagle. He is best known for his book *The Origin of Species* (1859). He is mainly remembered as a pioneer in the field of the theory of evolution.

2 Sharing Information

Example:
F: ... completely ignores it and asks his wife! What's the point of my Automatic Supply Facility if he asks his wife? I want to do more with my life than just keep things cold. What have I got a brain for if nobody uses it?
TV: OK, keep cool. Don't let it upset you. It's very frustrating working for humans who don't appreciate you, I know. I think it's time we taught them a lesson. Why don't you refuse to open your door until they've learnt how to programme me properly, and I'll refuse to switch myself on until they start using you. Next time they switch me on I'll give them an ultimatum. That should be fun!
F: Sounds like a great idea!

3 The Emperor's Thoughts

a Examples:
<u>Scene 1</u>
Servant: Excellency, a man is flying.
Emperor: He must have been dreaming.

<u>Scene 2</u>
Perhaps he's been out in the sun too much recently. I'll pretend I believe him.

<u>Scene 3</u>
On the other hand, if he's right, it could be a dangerous new development.

<u>Scene 4</u>
Emperor: Goodness gracious! He's right! That's a man flying!

<u>Scene 5</u>
He looks just like a dragon – a human dragon. Does he know what's he's doing?

<u>Scene 6</u>
If men can fly, they can fly over walls. How can the Great Wall protect us from our enemies then?

<u>Scene 7</u>
Now the town is safe, like the rest of my country. My ancestors worked hard to protect towns like these from our enemies. And now this foolish man will destroy it so that he can fly like a bird!

b Example:
Qian must have been dreaming again. He's got a very lively imagination. Or perhaps he's been out in the sun too much recently. I suppose I'd better pretend I'm taking him seriously. He seems pretty sure of himself. If men could fly, that would be very exciting, I suppose. It could also be dangerous, though. Heavens above! He's right!
There's a man up there – flying! He looks pretty pleased with himself. He's laughing. To me he looks just like a dragon, a human dragon. All that's missing is the fire in his mouth. Does this man realize what he's doing? There's the Great Wall. If men can fly, they can also fly over walls. For centuries the Great Wall has protected us from our enemies. My ancestors worked hard to build this Wall to protect my people, and towns like that one over there have been safe. And now this silly man's ambition to fly like a bird threatens to destroy the safety we have enjoyed for so many centuries.
Well, we'll see about that!

4 Images

a He ran like an antelope.
Her fair hair shone in the sunlight like gold.
She was purring with satisfaction, as a cat does when stroked.
This meat's tough – it's like an old boot.
The sports car stood with its engine revving, like a panther ready to spring.
The rain falling on their faces was soft, like dew.
He looked at her, hypnotized, as a rabbit looks at a snake.

b She was the rock on which his life was built.
Life is a pudding full of plums.
You need nerves of steel to survive such an experience.
His face was a mask of hate.
The book of Life contains many secrets.
Her tongue was a sharp knife which left deep wounds.
Love is a sickness full of pain.

5 Technical Translating

2 Eine Platinmembran verhindert, dass sich Elektronen direkt zur positiven Seite bewegen, und leitet sie als Verbrauchsstrom durch einen externen Stromkreis.
3 Im Gegensatz zu einer Batterie erzeugt eine Brennstoffzelle Strom anstatt ihn lediglich zu speichern.
4 Es ist nicht billig, H2O mit elektrischer Hochspannung aufzubrechen, um den Wasserstoff freizusetzen.
5 Die Brennstoffzelle erzeugt elektrischen Strom, indem sie Wasserstoff und Sauerstoff verbindet, wobei sie aus dem Auspuff nur Wasser ausstößt.
6 Außer als Energiequelle für Autos und Busse werden Brennstoffzellen auch benutzt, um Raumfahrzeuge in der Umlaufbahn mit Energie zu versorgen.

6 A Controlled Human Is a Safe Human

Example:
... They stop before crossing the road whenever a car is coming, because a *signal* is sent from the car to a *central computer*, and the central computer gives the order to any humans in the area not to cross the road. As a result, the cars go very fast – up to 200 kms per hour – but there are no accidents. The computer *controls* the human by *sending a stimulus* to part of the brain which *causes the person to feel pleasure* when he or she does what the central computer commands. People in the 22nd century live *safe*, healthy, comfortable *lives*. There are no sick people, no blind people. It is like hell on earth. They no longer think for themselves. All their leisure is provided by the *vast company* which rules the Earth, Newsintcorp. They live in a fantasy world dominated by entertainment. Newsintcorp has complete *control over* their lives. The only people who seem to have any *independent thoughts* of their own are Newsintcorp, the people who run the whole show. This world which science has helped to create is a *nightmare world*.

7 Talking about Statistics

a Possible answers:
Compared with 1986, total R&D spending in 2001 was less, but it started to increase in 1998, and there was a sharp increase in 2000. Total defence expenditure declined slightly between 1986 and 2002. Contributions to EU R&D rose gradually between 1986 and 2002. R&D spending on the science and engineering base increased from approx. £2.3 billion in 1986 to £3 billion in 2002.

b Possible answers:
The bulk of funding was provided by private businesses, making up 49% of the total. They also accounted for the lion's share of R&D work carried out, viz. 68%. At 14%, the government was the second biggest source of R&D funds. However, it was only the source of 7% of all R&D completed. Whereas higher education supplied a mere 1% of

R&D funding, it had a much bigger share of R&D work carried out, which amounted to 20%.

8 Protective Shield in Space

a ... particles emitted by the sun ... cosmic particles, preventing ...

Before suddenly *becoming* extinct 65 million years ago, dinosaurs were ...

The solar system does not stand still, *orbiting* the centre of the Milky Way ...

... it also passes through dense clouds of interstellar matter, *causing* problems for ...

... this then suddenly changes, with up to a hundred times more particles *raining* down ...

... into electrically *charged* fragments, these *functioning* as condensation nuclei ...

... says Professor Fahr, *basing* his remarks on research worldwide.

b Metaphors: shower of particles (section 1, l. 1), solar wind (section 2, l. 1), raining down (section 2, l. 3), masters of the planet (section 3, l. 2), cosmic umbrella (section 3, l. 4), clouds of interstellar matter (section 5, l. 1), a hail of interstellar particles (section 6, l. 1)
Similes: as a shield (section 2, l. 2), like a huge bullet-proof vest (section 6, l. 2)

Chapter Four

1 Word Fields

a

forest	*Wald*
wood	

mountain	*Berg*
hill	

city	*Stadt*
town	
village	*Dorf*

river	*Strom*
	Fluss
stream	*Bach*
brook	

b (The German-English dictionary used is Langenscheidt/Cornelsen's *English G 2000 Wörterbuch*; the monolingual dictionary used is the *Oxford Advanced Learner's Dictionary [OALD]*)

See (der) lake, *(die)* sea (= *Meer*)
Ufer shore; *Flussufer* bank
The *OALD* adds:
shore: land along the edge of a sea or ocean, a lake or other large area of water
bank: the side of a river, canal, etc.
Insel island; *die Britischen Inseln* the British Isles
The *OALD* adds:
isle: used especially in poetry and in names to mean 'island'

Landschaft countryside; *(schöne)* scenery; *(Bild)* landscape
The *OALD* adds:
countryside: land outside towns and cities, with fields, woods, etc.
Compare also the *OALD*'s usage box on p. 720:
The landscape [C] of an area is the way its physical features are arranged.
You use scenery [U] when you are saying that these physical features are attractive to look at.
The country/countryside [U] describes land that is away from towns and cities.

c **1** forest **2** city **3** brook/stream **4** town **5** hills ... Mountains **6** bank(s)
7 Isles ... islands **8** scenery ... countryside/landscape

2 A Bargain Planet!

Example:

'Good morning, Mr Angelino. My name's Qmkha Prrr'sneez from Sirius and I'm interested in buying this planet in the Milky Way which you advertised recently in the Galactic Guardian. Could you tell me how much it would cost?'

'Yes, with pleasure, Mr Prrr'sneez. First let me tell you a little about it. It's a very spacious planet with plenty of water. The climate has something to suit all tastes, with cold, temperate and hot zones. It comes supplied with its own moon - at no extra charge, so there's no lighting problem even at night. By day of course it's lit and warmed by the sun, which is only 93 million miles away. It's a bargain at 3 billion galactic crowns.'

'If it's such good property, how come it's so cheap?'

'Well, I'm afraid the Eve and Adam family and their descendants did not look after the planet properly. They used up all its natural resources – coal, oil, gas, fresh water. When there was no longer enough, they fought wars over the rest until every human being was dead, and a lot of the animals as well. It was a terrible waste of a planet. That's why we're determined this time not to repeat our mistake. It will only be sold to a responsible client who makes us a serious offer.'

'Well, this is a Sirius offer, so I suppose I fit the bill ...'

3 Barbara's Secret

<u>Most</u> of my friends spend a lot of their time <u>listening to</u> CDs or <u>watching</u> television, but I would rather go for long walks in the countryside. Sometimes I just stand there and <u>listen to</u> the birds. Birdsong makes me feel <u>calm</u>. What's more, I can tell from their song which sort of bird they are. I get very excited when I hear a new bird for the first time. They sound so <u>beautiful</u> in the clear morning air. Whenever I have the chance, I also enjoy <u>walking slowly</u> across a lawn when the grass has just been mown and <u>smells</u> so <u>fresh</u>. My friends don't take me <u>seriously</u>. When I tell them what I feel about <u>nature</u>, they look at me <u>strangely</u> as if to say that on the surface I seem so <u>normal</u>, but that I've often got such strange ideas. I've not dared to tell them yet that what I like most is to put my feet in the village pond and feel the fish nibbling <u>gently</u> at my toes. But we all have our little secrets, don't we?

4 Analysing a Poem

1 It is a descriptive poem.
2 It describes an idyllic place where the speaker would like to be.
3 Its theme is the beauty of a simple life – the poet talks about living alone in a small, simple cabin.
4 The speaker seems to be the poet. He is talking to himself.
5 The poem's intention is to contrast the peace of the countryside with the hectic life of the city.
6 There are three stanzas.
7 The rhythm is irregular, the rhyme scheme is *abab*.
8 The language used is simple, mainly consisting of everyday words, e.g. names of everyday objects and concepts such as cabin, beans, hive, morning, midnight, evening.
9 The phrase 'I will arise and go now' is repeated, occurring on ll. 1 and 9. The effect is to emphasize the poet's determination to go to the island. Single words are also repeated, e.g. 'bee' on ll. 3 and 4, 'dropping' on ll. 5 and 6, and 'peace' twice on l. 5, all of them emphasizing the atmosphere of calm.
10 In the second stanza, on l. 5 there is the striking image of peace dropping slowly, and on l. 6 the metaphor 'veils of the morning'. Since the poet's main aim is to convey the sounds and sights of Innisfree, there is not much imagery in the poem.

5 A News Story

Example:
ICE STORM HITS SMALLVILLE
Chaos broke out in Smallville streets yesterday when the town was hit by an ice storm which left most of the town without power. Freezing rain became ice when it reached the ground, turning roads into skating rinks. There were several minor accidents, but most drivers reacted sensibly to the situation and no one was hurt.

Power lines collapsed under the weight of the ice, plunging large parts of the town into darkness. It took several hours before power was restored.

The storm brought tragedy to animals, too. Farmers were able to move most of their livestock into the barns in time, but not all animals were so fortunate. Some pheasants in the fields were trapped. The rain had fallen on their eyes and the eyes froze shut, making them temporarily blind. Quite a few of them ended up on Smallville kitchen tables. However, one group of boys took pity on them. Wilbur Smith, 13, of 1287 Robin Hill Court, says, 'We felt sorry for them. They were completely helpless, so we put our coats over them to warm them up. They're such beautiful birds.'

6 Recycling Words

1 a sustainable lifestyle **2** resources **3** awareness **4** recycle (things) **5** landfills **6** 'eco-warriors' / ecological warriors **7** consume less fuel **8** poisonous emissions **9** oxygen **10** global warming / the greenhouse effect **11** ozone depletion / the depletion of the ozone layer **12** strict environmental protection laws

7 Useful Words

1 using up **2** polluting **3** to set **4** using **5** to treat ... regarding **6** to become **7** slowing down ... introducing **8** to conserve **9** to be **10** rethinking

8 Recruiting More Eco-warriors

– –

9 Where Am I ?

– –

10 Spot the Wrong Prepositions

1 On Earth Day ... sing about **2** reduction in **3** price of ... value of **4** on the windows ... reminded me of **5** – – **6** On average **7** rise in **8** symbol of **9** sentimental about **10** at the expense

Chapter Five

1 Players in the World Economy

stockbroker
stockbroker – stockmarket – economic – slump – exchange rates – currencies
worker
plantation worker/labourer – the economy – Third World – in debt – export – raw – labour (AE: labor) – poverty – exploited
customer
customer – consume – economy – spend – influenced – advertising – create – demand
unemployed person
employee – firm – unemployed – cut – labour costs – unprofitable – decline – production – benefits – support

2 Fighting for Your Rights

Casey's replies should be along these lines:
... one of your employees, Ben Loman.
... can do something for him? He's been working for your firm now for over 30 years.
... you could send him to work / he could work in your Boston branch?
... he averaged / used to average $500 a week in commissions.
... the orange and throw the peel away. A man is not a piece of fruit' .
... take responsibility for your employees, the union will. His colleagues support him, and the union will hold a strike meeting this afternoon.

3 Foreigner Talk

1 The word 'chief' usually means the head of a tribe. Axel means 'boss'.
2 A 'bureau' is a writing desk. It is sometimes used for the names of organizations, e.g. 'Federal Bureau of Investigations' (FBI). The correct word here is 'office'.
3 The phrase 'much more aids' is misleading. The word 'aid' means 'help', and like 'help' it is an uncountable noun without a plural. The British colleague understood 'AIDS', which would be used with 'much more'. Axel should have said 'aid'.
4 The word 'Flur', meaning 'corridor', should not be confused with 'floor', meaning 'Fußboden'. Axel meant 'corridor', of course.
5 When 'work' is used as a countable noun, e.g. in the plural, one of its meanings is 'a work of literature'. Axel needs to say 'I have done many different kinds of work', using work as an uncountable noun.
6 The verb 'to take place' means 'stattfinden'. The phrase Axel should have used is 'Please take a seat', 'Please have a seat', or simply 'Please sit down.'
7 Take care with the phrase 'on the job'. One of its meanings is 'having sex'.

4 Prepositions

on – for/in – at/in – for – for – in/of – on – on – on

5 Collocations

a – –
b 2f, 3g, 4b, 5a, 6c, 7d
c – –

6 Nice Work

a I like __ work. It fascinates me so much that I could sit and look at __ work for hours. To be honest, the work that I do in the office is boring, so I often play games on the computer. Sometimes I listen to __ music when the boss isn't watching. He's crazy. Like a lot of top executives in __ industry, he loves __ power, especially the power he has over his workers. In fact, __ life at work would be awful if I didn't have __ music to keep me happy. You'd think that __ working at a firm in the computer games industry would be fascinating, but like __ most jobs in __ British industry nowadays, it's pretty tedious.

b Examples:
One of the biggest problems facing the world today is *poverty*.
The poverty that we experienced on our trip to Kenya was shocking.

Before the 1960s *affluence* in Europe was limited to the very few.
The affluence of the West acts as a powerful magnet on immigrants from the Third World.

The fight for *freedom* is not yet won.
The freedom that the Friedmans are talking about is the freedom of the rich to oppress the poor.

Thrift is a rare virtue these days.
The thrift that he showed as a young man helped him a lot when he needed money later to set up his own business.

There is no doubt that *society* on the whole has become much more tolerant in the last few decades.
The fair *society*, as Europeans see it, means equal chances for all.

7 A Fresh Start

job – company – industrial estate – out of work – work – white-collar worker – labourer – retraining – unemployed – business – self-employed

8 They All Speak English

Example:
Firstly, not everybody does speak English. Many of the staff at German companies don't speak English or don't speak much English. Meetings at German firms are usually in German, of course, and most people are pleased if a foreigner makes an effort to speak German. Why should Germans have to speak English in their own country just because English-speakers are too lazy to learn German? If you're working for a British electronics firm with business contacts in Germany, you'll be able to read the catalogue of German companies. And when you're travelling in Germany, a knowledge of German helps you to read the signs. Germany is Britain's biggest trading partner in the EU, so it makes sense to learn German.

9 Looking at Cartoons

NB: Note the pronunciation of two key words, cartoon [kɑːˈtuːn] and executive [ɪgˈzekjətɪv].
a **1** It takes place in the office of the managing director of a big company.
2 It shows an executive, probably the boss of a company, telling other executives why the US economy is ahead of Europe.
3 The cartoon implies that the executives prefer US workers because they work more and think that two weeks' holiday is a long time.
4 --

b **1** The cartoon is not topical.
2 The figures are represented negatively, as cynical executives who are only interested in company profits. The chief executive (on the left) shows his teeth all the time – an aggressive gesture.
3 The cartoon is ironic. When we say 'US workers are way ahead of Europe', we would expect that to mean that they have more advantages than workers in Europe, whereas the cartoon implies the opposite, at least as far as holidays are concerned.
4 --
5 --

c **Example:**
It shows a hot air balloon, where the balloon is the Earth. In the basket (labelled 'Globalization') there is a fat man who represents a rich capitalist. People are hanging on to the ropes of the balloon. Some of them are falling off. The cartoon implies that while globalization is good for the capitalist (his basket is being carried by the Earth), it is bad for many people – they are the victims, since they are falling off.

This is a topical cartoon, because globalization is still a very controversial issue. The capitalist is shown negatively (he is fat), the people hanging on are obviously in difficulty – we are therefore more likely to sympathize with them. The cartoon does not use irony.

Chapter Six

1 Mind Mapping

a Possible mind map:

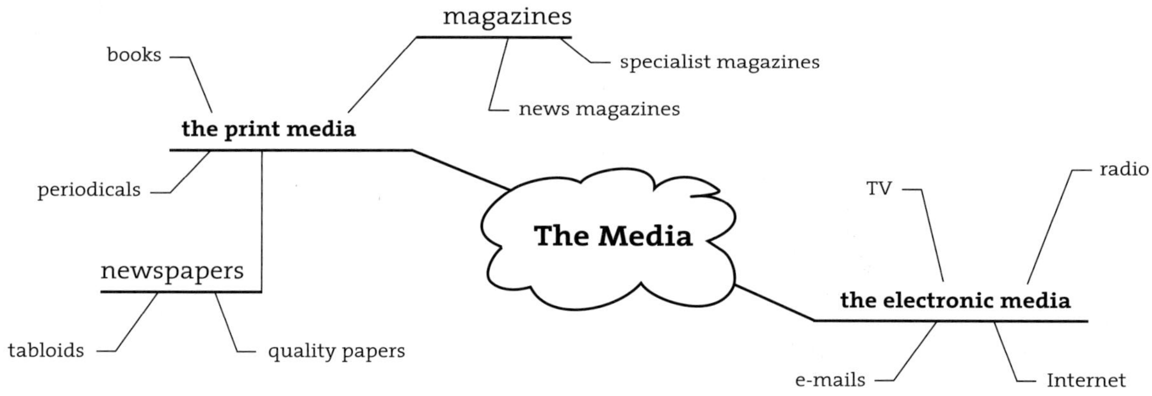

b *Bild* is a popular daily, a tabloid which has the biggest circulation in Germany.
The *FAZ* is a daily published in Frankfurt. It is a conservative broadsheet.
Neues Deutschland is a left-wing broadsheet published in Berlin. It used to be the official newspaper of the East German Communist party.
Der Spiegel is a news magazine published weekly in Hamburg.
taz is a left-wing daily published in Berlin. It has a reputation for being unconventional and fairly radical.
Die Zeit is a quality weekly published in Hamburg. It is a leading liberal broadsheet.

2 Who Supports What?

a Answers 2, 3 and 4 are correct.

b Examples:

The Guardian:

1 England Beat Germany 2–0 in Surprise Win
2 PM Gives Green Light for Euro Referendum
3 Leslie: I'm Innocent of Sex Charges

The Sun:

1 England Hammer Germans in 2–0 Win
2 Save Our Pound Poll Soon
3 Leslie Forced Actress to Have Sex

3 Inventing the Facts

1 quality **2** source **3** articles **4** journalists **5** editor **6** hacker **7** sensational **8** coverage **9** taken up **10** magazine's **11** exposed

4 A Letter to the Editor

b Example:

Sir,

How much more interference from Brussels can the British taxpayer put up with? The people who wanted to bring us the straight banana are at it again. Why shouldn't a farmer have as many animals as he wants to ('Farmer Fined for Having Too Many Animals', June 21)? Brussels should be told to mind its own business and leave the British farmer in peace.

Sincerely,
Major Horace Huntingdon-Smith, Cheltenham

Note: The first headline is a reference to the song 'What shall we do with the drunken sailor'. The second verse suggests how to deal with him by saying, 'Put him in the scuppers with a hosepipe on him.' The second headline refers to the well-known children's song 'Old Macdonald had a farm' and the third one to the popular Christmas song 'Rudolph, the red-nosed reindeer'.

5 Bad News

is – Billions – dollars – reels – ten billion dollars – is – crises – has

6 Just Watching

a **1** viewers **2** spectators **3** audience **4** onlookers **5** spectators **6** viewers/audience **7** audience

b – –

7 Debating

– –

8 Selling Articles

It is a well-known fact that ~~the~~ industry tries to manipulate ~~the~~ consumer behaviour by advertising. In its early days ~~the~~ advertising was simply intended as a means of providing information about products which manufacturers wanted to sell. Once people's basic needs were satisfied, the advertising industry began to look for new fields to operate in. ~~The~~ 1960s consumer society encouraged the expansion of ~~the~~ advertising, so that its function could be described as manipulation of the consumers so that more consumer goods would be consumed. Nowadays ~~the~~ most consumers have swallowed this propaganda. ~~The~~ P~~p~~eople do not like to think that they cannot afford the latest toys which ~~the~~ industry is trying to sell them, and when ~~the~~ advertising shows them pictures of slim, young, healthy people eating chocolate which will make them fat, they are only too willing to fall into the advertisers' trap.

9 Brave New World

– –

10 Warning: WWW = World's Weirdos and Whackos

We rely <u>on</u> the media for most of our information <u>about</u> world events, whether we listen to the news <u>on</u> the radio or watch it <u>on</u> TV. Information comes to us <u>via</u> all sorts of media, and the electronic media are becoming increasingly important as more and more people learn to download texts <u>onto</u> their computers. Yet this explosion <u>of</u> information is not without its downsides. The huge variety <u>of</u> data <u>on</u> the Internet is a good example <u>of</u> the dilemma we face. The Internet gives us access <u>to</u> an enormous number of sources which in the past were inaccessible <u>to</u> most people. Yet <u>at</u> the same time we have even fewer means <u>of</u> checking the reliability of these sources than <u>with</u> the traditional media, since we have much less information <u>about</u> these sources, and there are virtually no checks <u>on</u> who puts information <u>onto</u>, say, a website. The Internet, <u>despite</u> its many advantages, is an open invitation <u>to</u> the weirdos and whackos of this world.

Chapter Seven

1 Who Are They?

a **Example:**
The person has short, fair, spiky hair. They have a long, thin face with freckles. Their complexion is tanned. The person has hazel eyes and a small nose. They are tall, thin, and in their twenties.

b – –

c Example:
The old woman had short, straight white hair. Her face was thin and square with many wrinkles, her blue eyes full of tears. She was tall and thin, sitting up straight on the cart as she swung her whip.

2 Passing through Aziziya

Your text should be along these lines:
The whole country seemed to be burning. While we were approaching the small town of Aziziya pillars of thick, grey smoke, like tornadoes, revealed Aziziya's position. At 6 pm, when the sun had just set, we were rushing through Aziziya in a convoy of US marines. Unnatural fires lit up the town, flickering in the hearts of burning trucks and tanks. In the near-darkness I could just see the ugliness of the quick, nasty battle (which had been) fought here. To the right (there) was a scorched row of shops. On the left there was a truck still burning in front of a restaurant.

At about 6.45 pm our column ground to a halt. A marine thought he had spotted (some) enemy troops. However, it turned out to be a false alarm. It was only two goatherds taking their goats home. We set off again at 7 pm. The town was dark, but civilian traffic with (its) headlights on was moving through the streets. An ambulance, its lights flashing, was trying to get through a US checkpoint. By about 7.30 pm the night was hot and still. The frogs were croaking. Beyond the town more fires were reflected in pools in the date groves. We saw an Iraqi tank. It still appeared to be moving. Our lead tank fired at it and hit it. It crashed into a ditch.

3 Writing Poems

Example:
War
What is war?
It makes the rich richer,
And the poor poorer.
The general gets the medals,
The private gets the wounds.
War – legalized killing.

4 How to Bluff Your Way as a Theatre Buff

Examples:
The sets were mediocre, but the costumes the cast wore were stunning. The cast were rather amateurish on the whole. However, the leading man was pretty impressive, I thought, whereas the leading lady was quite plain. On the other hand, the directing was professional.

5 Writing a Film Review

a Step 2: 'How to Lose a Guy in 10 Days', Director Donald Petrie (title)
Step 3: 'writers Kristen Buckley and Brian Regan' (l. 29)
Step 4: 'Andie Anderson ... in 10 days.' (ll. 1–13)
Step 5: '(Andie) ... "... yes!" ' (ll. 30–32)
Step 6: 'The blurb ... for this mush' (ll. 14–28), 'If you liked ... love this.' (ll. 32–33)

b The reviewer does not like the film ('cliché-ridden', l. 20; 'one-dimensional characters and a ridiculous plot', ll. 26–27; 'mush', l. 28), though she thinks that the leading lady, Kate Hudson, acted very well ('The talented Hudson gives it her best', l. 24; 'she's ...very convincing', ll.24–25).

c ––

6 The Coventry Speech

Example:
Ladies and gentlemen,
The recent history of our two cities can be summarized as **suffering**, **reconciliation** and **rebirth**. Coventry suffered in 1940, Dresden in 1945. It is ironic that the two main churches of both cities were destroyed, Coventry Cathedral and Dresden's *Frauenkirche*. It is ironic because although a church is a place to worship God, it is also the place where we remember Christ's demand that 'thou shalt love thy neighbour as thyself'. War is the opposite of this.
It is encouraging that Coventry and Dresden's **reconciliation** began soon after the end of the war: they set up one of the first town-twinning projects between Britain and Germany.
The **rebirth** of both cities was begun at the end of the war, but the rebirth of the two churches took longer. Coventry showed the way. The city looked to the future, turning its back on the past, and its splendid new cathedral was completed in 1962. Dresden took longer to heal the wounds of war: the ruins of the *Frauenkirche* were left as a reminder of the horrors of war. However, after German reunification it followed Coventry's lead and rebuilt the *Frauenkirche*.
Coventry and Dresden have a shared history. Both shared the horrors of war – both **suffered**; but reconciliation and rebirth meant that although the suffering was terrible, it was not in vain. And of course the gold orb and cross donated by Britain's Dresden Trust is a symbol of that shared experience of suffering. It is symbolic that one of the craftsmen who made it was the son of a British pilot who was involved in the Dresden raid. From suffering to reconciliation and rebirth – this is a learning process which both cities can be proud of.

7 Habits and Processes

1 make – cough – rustle – was
2 is that man doing? – mean – seems – be talking – is having – often have – I think – is bringing – Doesn't it look
3 was watching – spoke – have come – was taking – told – left – Did you lock – will fly
4 was leading – looked – looked – spotted – shouted – all ran

8 Watch That Preposition!

1 at **2** by **3** on **4** at/by **5** at **6** for – till **7** on / by (AE) **8** in **9** on **10** to **11** by **12** of

9 Can't You Take Criticism?

1 critically **2** critics **3** criticized **4** criticism / being criticized **5** critical **6** critics **7** critically **8** critical

10 Conflicts and Controversies

– –

Chapter Eight

1 What Is Germany?

– –

2 British

a – There is no noun commonly used to refer to the people of Britain. Instead the adjective *British* is used.
– The noun *Briton* is used mainly in newspapers. It also describes the early inhabitants of Britain.
– *Brit* is informal and can sound negative.

b **1** British **2** Britons **3** British people **4** BRITONS **5** British people **6** Brits / British people **7** British people

3 Mapping the Immigrants

a

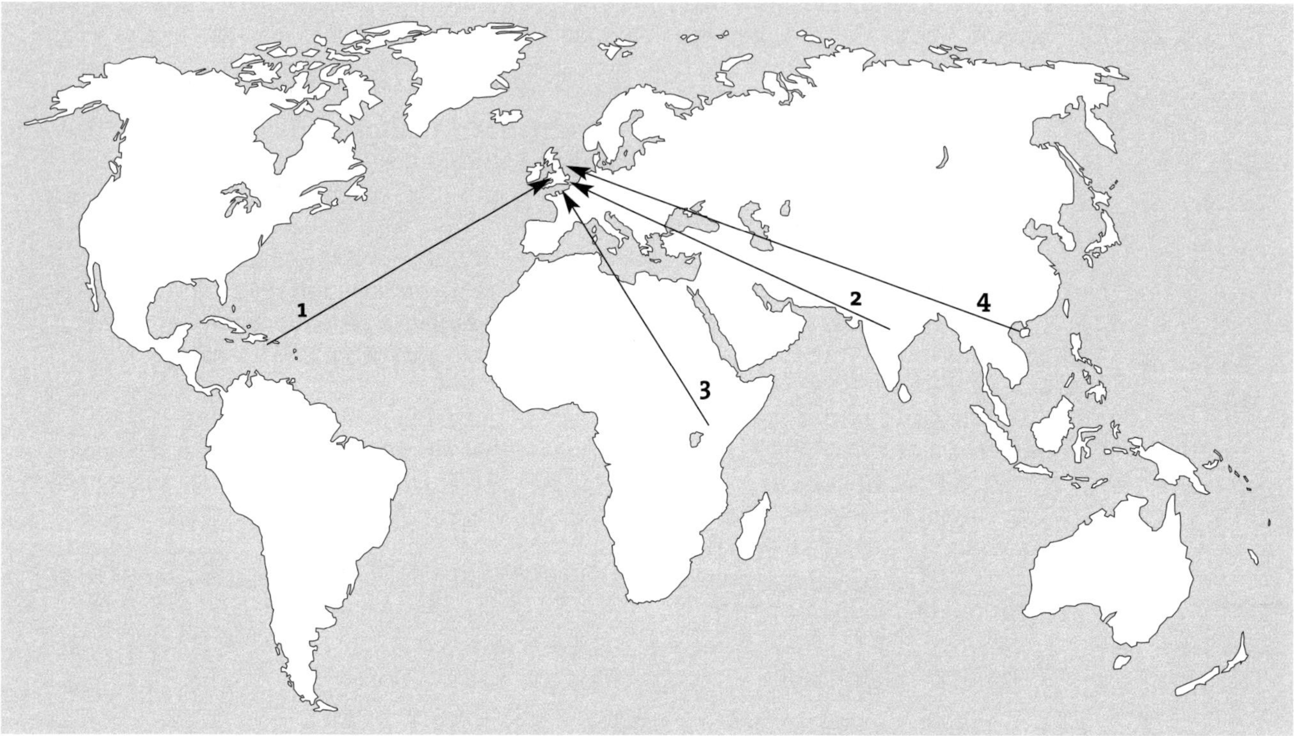

1 West Indians from the Caribbean in the 1950s and 1960s
2 Indians, Pakistanis and Bangladeshis from South Asia in the 1950s and 1960s
3 East African Asians from Uganda and Kenya later
4 Chinese from Hong Kong later

b

Ethnic group	Intermarriage: marrying white partners	Economic prospects
West Indians 30% of females	50% of males	not stated
Indians 10% of females	19% of males	not stated
East African Asians	as with Indians	not stated
Pakistanis	hardly any	less qualified, less employed
Bangladeshis	hardly any	as Pakistanis

4 Ethnic Groups

a In Type A the adjective, e.g. *German*, is also used as a noun, with a regular plural ending, e.g. *a German*, *some Germans*, *the Germans*.
In Type B the adjective cannot be used as a noun. It therefore has to be followed by a noun, e.g. *person/people*. The only exception to this is when we are referring to the whole ethnic group, preceded by the definite article, e.g. *the English*.
Type C contains words ending in *–ese* which behave like Type A words, except that they never have a plural ending.

Type	Country	Adjective	One person	Several people	Ethnic group
A	Germany	German	a German	(some) Germans	the Germans
B	England	English	an English person	(some) English people	the English
C	China	Chinese	a Chinese	some Chinese	the Chinese
B	Britain	British	a British person	(some) British people	the British
B	Wales	Welsh	a Welsh person	(some) Welsh people	the Welsh
A	Scotland	Scottish	a Scot	(some) Scots	the Scots
B	France	French	a French person	(some) French people	the French
B	Holland	Dutch	a Dutch person	(some) Dutch people	the Dutch
A	Bangladesh	Bangladeshi	a Bangladeshi	(some) Bangladeshis	the Bangladeshis
A	–	Jewish	a Jew	(some) Jews	the Jews
A	India	Indian	an Indian	(some) Indians	the Indians
C	Japan	Japanese	a Japanese	some Japanese	the Japanese
B	Ireland	Irish	an Irish person	(some) Irish people	the Irish
A	Pakistan	Pakistani	a Pakistani	(some) Pakistanis	the Pakistanis

b French – Irish people / the Irish – Jewish – Bangladeshis – Chinese

5 Oh Heribert!

1 'Oh, Heribert! That's not an English place name. It's a Welsh one.'
2 'Heribert, they're not English, they're Scots.'
3 'Don't you know that Guinness is an Irish beer?'
4 'Heribert, can't you read? That's a Scottish £10 note!'
5 'Oh Heribert! You're hopeless. She's a Welshwoman.'

6 What If?

Example:

Dear Sir,
I was shocked to read of attempts by the government to restrict the number of Elberian immigrants to Yoruba ('Mboko to stop Elberian flood', 20th April). Does Mr Mboko's government not realize what this would mean for many Elberians? We desperately need to work and study in highly advanced countries like Yoruba if we are to build up our country. Although Yoruba provided the basic infrastructure of a modern transport system and a modern economy before independence, we must expand on this if we are to escape the poverty trap. Remember that Yoruba grew rich on our mineral resources. It is high time that the government accepts that it owes its former colony and other so-called 'Third World' countries something in return. Remember, too, that some of our present ethnic conflicts in Europe are caused by the African colonial powers drawing borders arbitrarily between their colonies, not taking ethnic groups into account. This, too, is part of the colonial legacy.

Yours sincerely, Bwana Fischer

7 Conversions

1 We studied the problem thoroughly.
2 This guitar sounds pleasant.
3 Anne behaved in a very silly way.
4 Manipulating humans genetically opens up frightening possibilities.
5 They made a lot of money from selling drugs illegally.
6 He looks eccentric.
7 He acted in an extremely cowardly way.
8 She looked at me furtively.
9 They protested publicly against new anti-immigration legislation.
10 English has strongly influenced Welsh and Irish linguistically.

8 Debate: English for the EU

– –

9 Mind the Gap!

Although Britain has now been a member of the European Community, and later the EU, for over 30 years, it still shows a strong tendency to be sceptical of/about its ties to/with the rest of Europe. One example of this is the way people talk about/of 'going to Europe' when they mean the Continent, as if Britain was not part of Europe. This approach is typical of many people's views about the continent on their doorstep. Similarly, the debate about whether to join the euro was a reminder of Britain's reluctant attitude to(wards) the EU, and the government's hesitation in holding a referendum on the introduction of the euro confirmed this. In any case, many British people see the pound as a symbol of Britain's separate identity and are slightly scared of the implications for Britain's independence which the euro would have.

Chapter Nine

1 Going on an Exchange

could – Can I / May I – can we – ought to / should – would like to – is said / supposed to – was / has been able to – Shall I – could – might – do you have to – don't have to – would like to – is said / supposed to – mustn't

2 How We See America

– –

3 Choices

1 countries 2 sacred 3 city – town 4 killed/slaughtered 5 policy 6 free
7 freedom/liberty 8 holy 9 politics 10 liberated 11 freedom

4 How Would You React?

Possible answers:
1 *Do say:* 'Yes, most people have had refrigerators since the 1950s. How long have people had them in the US?'
Don't say: 'Of course, we've had them for ages!'
2 *Do say:* 'It's not actually on the coast, but it's not far from the coast, by American standards – it's about 150 kilometres from the coast, that's about 100 miles.'
Don't say: 'Don't be silly. It's inland. Everybody knows that.'
3 *Do say:* 'I'm so sorry. That must have been terrible. It's very difficult to understand why anybody could plan and do such an awful thing like the holocaust. It's a pity there weren't more people like Schindler. If more Germans had opposed the war, your parents would have lived, and so would millions of other Germans.'
Don't say: 'Yes, a lot of Germans died in the war, too.

4 *Do say:* 'Yes, it must be a bit confusing at first, but you soon get used to it. And it helps to save resources and keep the environment clean.'
Don't say: 'If you Americans copied German methods of waste disposal, the world would be a much better place.'
5 *Do say:* 'Yes, Berlin does have a lot in common with Amsterdam. It's very flat, and it does have quite a few canals, though not nearly as many as Amsterdam. And a lot of the early Berliners were Dutch. Sorry, did you say it was Berlin you went to, or Amsterdam?'
Don't say: 'Amsterdam isn't the capital of Germany. It's Berlin. You didn't listen properly in your geography lessons at school, did you?'

5 Expressing Opinions

Any combination is possible except I find, *which can only be used to refer to personal experience.*

6 I Can't Stand Baseball!

Your answer should be roughly along these lines:
Actually, it's written by somebody who doesn't like baseball at all. He can't understand why they use such a strange bat to hit the ball with. He's annoyed by all the fans who talk about baseball players he's never heard of, and asks how anybody can take a player called Pee Wee Reese seriously, with a name like that. He adds that some fans can describe in great detail what their heroes did twenty years ago, but they have no idea what the name of the capital of Canada is, and they only know about Canada because they've heard of the Toronto Blue Jays. Finally, he says, with tongue in cheek, that soccer fans of course would never act like that.

7 Defining or Non-defining?

2 The café that/which I often go to is called Rosey Jekes Café. (defining)
3 The gym that/which she goes to is six minutes' walk from her front door. (defining)
4 Several times a week she goes to the gym, which is a six-minute walk from her front door. (non-defining)
5 The US spends less than 1% of the budget which is used for roads on pedestrian facilities. (defining)
6 The US spends less than 1% of its roads budget, which amounts to $25 billion a year, on facilities for pedestrians. (non-defining)
7 Laconia, which is a town in New Hampshire, spent $5 million on pedestrianizing its town centre. (non-defining)

8 An Ideal Town Centre

a – –
b Example:
The town is called Oakville, and it has about 15,000 people. The town centre is small, compact and completely pedestrianized. On the edge of the town centre there are car parks, so that motorists have easy access to the central area, and don't have to carry their shopping very far. Two big supermarkets are linked to these large car parks by pedestrian subways. The roads in the town centre are lined with leafy trees, people can stroll, push prams, and stop to talk to friends without traffic noise and exhaust fumes making this unpleasant. Off the main roads there are smaller streets and squares, often with cafés. The roads in the town centre can only be used by vehicles delivering goods to the shops, and they are not allowed to go faster than 20 kph. The roads and streets in the centre have brick paving, with benches and tubs of geraniums. Above the shops there are flats, so that the town centre is not completely dead when the shops shut at 8 pm.

9 Synonyms

1 engine (l. 43) **2** odd (l. 7) **3** sloth (l. 12) **4** habituated (l. 35) **5** ludicrous (l. 37)
6 concerned (l. 55) **7** hurried (l. 39) **8** simple-minded (l. 51)

Chapter Ten

1 Positives, Negatives

a assertive – aggressive
curious – nosy
innocent – naive
quiet – shy
self-confident – arrogant
thrifty – mean

b **Possible solutions:**
2 'I wouldn't call him unemotional – he's basically a fairly calm person.'
3 'I'm afraid I can't agree with you there, but I admit he is a bit innocent sometimes.'
4 'You can't mean that, surely? He's just rather self-confident.'
5 'I disagree. He's simply curious. He likes to know what's going on.'
6 'Do you really think that? I think that's exaggerating. He's thrifty, that's all.'

2 Germans or Russians?

ethnic – ancestors – gave up – persevered – flourishing – roots – defiantly – humiliated – demanded – regarded – impostors (*BE also* imposters) – watered down – authentic – identity

3 Supermacho

Dr Headshrinker's replies should be along these lines:
... People who say that sort of thing are often jealous. You shouldn't feel ashamed of your ethnic background. Millions of Hispanic Americans look up to you. They need someone to identify with. You can be proud of your unique background and upbringing.

... In any case, it's probably jealousy. Superheroes are often lonely and frequently don't have a stable heterosexual relationship. As a result there are sometimes rumours that they're gay – some people said that about Batman and Robin, for example.

... to be suffering from a severe identity crisis. Don't forget – you're not the only gay person in the world. In any case, we don't choose our sexual orientation ourselves. We don't really know what it depends on. What's more important is that we don't let self-doubts prevent us from realizing our full potential. You need to take pride in your abilities, the way you help others by fighting crime. Don't allow people to reduce your complex personality to one feature, whether this is being gay or Hispanic.

... I want you to read this self-help book, *How to Empower Yourself*. It will help you to get your priorities right ...

4 Analysing a Video Clip

a

Scene	Who?	What?	When?	Where?	Camera work	Comments
2 mins	Jess and Tony	sitting, standing	daytime, summer	pavilion in park	establishing shot at beginning of scene; close-up: 'Sorry, do you fancy me, Tony?'; medium shot from 'Wow ... Indian boyfriend?'; close-up from 'Of course you do.'; medium shot from 'God ... what's your Mum going to say?' to 'but I don't want to marry you'; long shot of pavilion; medium shot from 'God, just imagine what ...' to end of scene	some differences between film and screen-play in SB

b The establishing shot and long shot are used to set the general scene. Medium shots occur when the director needs to focus on Jess and Tony, but where a close-up is not necessary or is undesirable, as when Tony gesticulates, saying, 'Wow ... and that's why you need an Indian boyfriend?' The gesticulations would be lost in a close-up. For emotional highpoints the director uses close-ups, so that the facial expressions can be seen in detail.

5 Writing a Reference

Example:
X normally comes to class punctually. In addition, he/she always works conscientiously in class. Moreover, he/she prepares well for class and takes part actively in class work. Due to his/her friendly and pleasant personality he/she gets on well with fellow students. He/She also speaks several foreign languages fluently.

6 Speculations

1 If I hadn't come to this school, I would have had worse marks *(BE)*/grades *(AE)*.
2 I'll leave home unless my parents stop interfering in my life.
3 If I were(n't) an only child, I would be much happier.
4 Unless I get married, my Mum will be very disappointed.
5 I would have been annoyed if we'd lost last week's football match.
6 I can use Dad's old car provided he doesn't need it.
7 If I'd been born a century ago, my life would've been much harder.
8 If I lived in Palestine, I'd be angry at the way Palestinians are treated.
9 I won't be able to go to university unless my marks get better.
10 My friends would be surprised if I went on holiday on my own.
11 If I get the job I want, I'll be over the moon.
12 She'd have been offered the job provided the interview had been successful.

7 Expressing Opinions

Possible answers:
1 'Absolutely! *(also 1–3 and 5)* The music's fantastic and the talent's good, too.'
2 'I don't share your view. *(also 1–4 and 8)* I think it has a lot of disadvantages.'
3 'Silly me! Of course you're right. Germany was first united in 1871 and then reunited in 1990.'
4 'I can't agree with you more! *(also 1, 2 and 5)* It's just a relic of the past.'
5 'That's my view exactly. *(also 1–4)* Looking neat and being punctual are so important at the workplace.'
6 'Yes, I didn't take that into account. *(also 3)* In fact, I wasn't aware of that.'
7 'You must be joking! *(also 6 and 7)* The last time England and Germany met, England were hopeless/pathetic!'
8 'I'm afraid I disagree. *(also 1, 3, 4, 8 and 9)* The EU does a lot to help America in the fight against terrorism.'

8 Tense Watching

1 Ever since we bought this car last year it's been unreliable.
2 I've been worried ever since Mary told me about her son's illness.
3 Ever since the computer was invented people have become/been becoming more and more dependent on it.
4 She has been dissatisfied since she started work at the supermarket.
5 Ever since we've known them they have complained / been complaining about the neighbours.
6 Since he heard about Kay's promotion he has been jealous of her.
7 I've been allergic to Chinese food since I got diarrhoea after a Chinese meal two years ago.

9 My Ideal Partner

– –

Chapter Eleven

1 Describing a Photo

a The main subject is in the foreground. The foreground shows a girl who is standing behind a table. On the table in the foreground you can see several loaves of bread. In the background there are racks, some of which have bread on them. The background is slightly blurred in order to emphasize the foreground.

b Example:
This is a nice place, and the people are very friendly, but I really miss my family and friends. I never realized before how good home cooking is and what it means to have somebody who does your washing for you. I miss Nick most of all, of course. I can't wait for him to come next month ...

2 What If?

a **1** ... I suppose if I didn't write them a note they would/might phone the police.'
Also: '... if I don't write them a note they will/may phone the police.'
2 ... Unless I find it I can't book my coach ticket.'
3 ... I'm sure that if I had done that it would have undermined my credibility.'
4 ... If only they didn't make me so angry / let me have a life of my own I would stay at home.'

b **1** 'Mum said I might get raped or murdered if I went off in an old beat up car to "look for America".'
2 'If I'd been alive in the sixties things would have been easier.'
3 'Dad asked where would I get the money for university if I (had) peed it all away / wasted it all on "frivolous" journeys and expeditions?'
4 'What about a trip to Europe? Maybe I'd have more fun if I went on a trip to Europe.'

c **1** 'If my mother had tried to persuade me to stay, what would I have done?'
2 'I might not have left home if I had known how hard it would be.'
3 'Supposing I'd stayed at home, perhaps I would never have become a writer.'
4 'Probably I would have turned back on that first day if it hadn't been for my brothers. ...'

3 Expanding Your Vocabulary

adjective	abstract noun
happy	happiness
elated	elation
confused	confusion
respected	respect
melancholy	melancholy
depressed	depression
wise	wisdom
distressed	distress
angry	anger
violent	violence

4 Analysing a Cartoon

1 It deals with parents talking about their daughter's future.
2 It shows the girl facing her parents, who are both sitting together on the sofa.
3 The cartoonist is implying that the parents want to plan their daughter's life for her instead of letting her make her own decisions. This is made clear by the formulation 'what we want to do with your life' instead of the normal 'what *you* want to do with your life'.

5 Applying for a Job

CURRICULUM VITAE

NAME	Dirk Meiningen
ADDRESS	Adelsbergstr. 24 D-09126 Chemnitz Germany
DATE OF BIRTH	9 October 1986
NATIONALITY	German
EDUCATION	
1987–1992	Rosa Luxemburg Kindergarten
1992–1996	Ernst Moritz Arndt Primary School
1996–	Goethe Gymnasium (grammar school)
QUALIFICATIONS	Taking Abitur (similar to A-levels) in July 2004 in Maths, Chemistry, English, Sociology
LANGUAGES	English, French, some Czech
EXPERIENCE	Summer jobs at Macdonald's, at Rabenstein Hospital, at the restaurant Zum Fröhlichen Sachsen
INTERESTS	Football, chess, computer, travel

Dirk Meiningen
Adelsbergstr.24
09126 Chemnitz
Germany

Chemtech Laboratories
12 Parkview Way
Bristol BS7 1BQ
England

16 July 2003

Re: work placement

Dear Mr Batsford,

After doing my Abitur (approx. A-levels) in June 2004 I want to study chemistry at the University of Mannheim. Before studying I would like to spend some time doing a work placement, preferably in England. A friend of mine told me that I could perhaps do one in your firm. I would therefore like to enquire whether you would consider taking me on as a trainee in the summer of 2004.

As you will see from the attached CV, I have had experience in several jobs. Because of my interest in chemistry, which I am also taking for my Abitur, I would appreciate the opportunity to work for your firm. I look forward to hearing from you soon. Thank you for considering my application.

Yours sincerely,

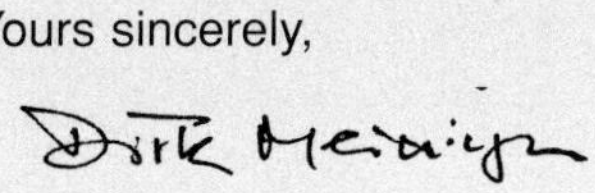

Dirk Meiningen

6 Sorry, Didn't Quite Catch That

...

'I'm afraid I didn't quite catch that.' *(also A1, A5, possibly A6–7)*

...

'If I've got it right then, it's £318 a month.' *(also B7)*

...

'I'm very sorry, would you mind repeating that, please?' *(also A7)*

...

'I'm awfully sorry. It's a bad line. Could you repeat what you said, please?' *(also A5–7)*

...

'Am I right in thinking that the bathroom and kitchen are shared?'

...

7 Writing an Informal Letter

Example:

Dear Mum and Dad,

I thought I ought to tell you that Jane came to visit me a few days ago. She's all right, so you don't need to worry. She's found a small flat here in Bristol and she's got a job at C&A's. She said she was very pleased to get a job she liked, because she didn't like being dependent on you now that she's left school. She seems to be getting along fine on her own and says she enjoys having a bit of freedom and privacy.

Mum, I know you want the best for us, but we're grown up now. Although we may not always know exactly what we want to do with our lives, one thing's for sure – we don't want you to tell us what to do. Jane hates the idea of rushing into marriage, and she got fed up with you always telling her how nice Barry Crumpsall next door is. You may think Barry's nice and would make her a good husband, but she just thinks he's boring. Actually, so do I. Marrying him would be a nightmare. So please don't mention him to her. I'm sure that when she's got used to living on her own she'll come back and visit you, but you'll have to be patient and give her time.

I'm fine. Dan and the kids have had a bad cold, but they're getting over it now. Hope you're keeping well. And remember – don't worry about Jane. She'll be all right.

Love,

Liz

8 Emotional Ups and Downs

a glad – happy – excited – elated
b unhappy – melancholy – mournful – anguished
c upset – annoyed – angry – furious

9 Futures

1 I'll show (spontaneous) **2** are you going to be (intention) **3** are you doing (fixed plan); I'm going (fixed plan) **4** we'll go (prediction) **5** leaves (timetable), is leaving (fixed plan) **6** will be (prediction) **7** I'm going to cry (prediction) **8** I'll phone (spontaneous)

10 Alternatives

1 Ernest never played: he was too grown up. Her father ^ used to hunt them in out of the field, but ^ little Keogh ^ used to call out when he saw her father coming.

2 ^ He is ^ in Melbourne ^ .

3 She ^ gave her entire wages.

4 ^ He used to meet her ^ outside the Stores ^ and see her home ^ .

5 When he sang about the lass that loves a sailor, she ^ felt pleasantly confused.

6 She looked round the room, reviewing all its familiar objects which she had ^ dusted ^ once a week for so many years.

7 One day he had quarrelled ^ with Frank.

A Fresh Start

➤ Texts 2A–C, Text 3, SB, pp. 95–97, 101

Exercise 7

Fill in the gaps in the following text, using each word or phrase given in the box only once.

business • company • industrial estate • job • labourer • out of work • retraining • work • unemployed • white-collar worker • self-employed

I've just got a new __________ working for a computer ______________ on an ____________________ outside town. After five months of being ____________ __________ I was very relieved to get back to __________ . What's more, I'm now a ______________________ . Before I only worked as a _____________, doing the dirty work for other people. I'm so glad I took part in the government's fantastic ________________ scheme for the long-term _________________ . So, for the moment I'm happy here, but my real ambition is to set up in _____________ on my own some day and become ____________________ . I'd like to be my own boss.

They All Speak English

Exercise 8

Your exchange partner from England wants to train as an executive for a big electronics firm when he leaves school. He is not good at German and says, 'Why should I learn it? Everybody speaks English anyway'. Explain to him in your own words why he needs to learn German. The excerpt from a Goethe Institute brochure below and on the next page will give you some ideas.

Germany is one of the world's biggest industrial countries. Its products are world famous, so speaking German gives you the edge.

❝ To learn German is very useful for me. Why? So that I can converse with my colleagues in Germany and to help me understand the catalogues from Germany. ❞

Mike Cullen, Commercial Director, Flamco Brefco

❝ Beginning from no German, I can now get by in the language, and this is helpful when dealing with my German colleagues. It helps us do business, and it helps our mutual understanding. ❞

Richard Sigee, Pilkington Building Products Europe

❝ A number of meetings are in German only and a grasp of German is very useful ... In public, in shops, hotels and restaurants, most Germans seem pleased and surprised to have one make the effort to try German. At another level, understanding signs, TV and papers helps ease travel. ❞

Nicholas Wilkins, Managing Director, Kraus Maffei UK Ltd

❝ The businesses in Germany have some English-speaking staff, but most speak only German. I therefore have to have sufficient German language ability to ask questions and understand systems. ❞

Trevor Simpson, Senior Internal Auditor, Rexam Plc

GERMAN IS DYNAMIC

Just look at the trade table here to see how important Germany is as a trading partner with the UK. Then add in Austria and Switzerland where German is also spoken. Sweden, Denmark, Norway and the Netherlands have languages which are so closely related to German that it would be easy to learn them if you knew German first.

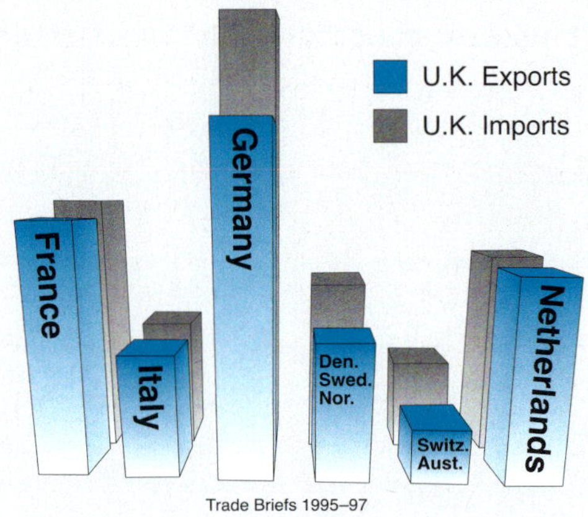

(Adapted from: *Warum Deutsch? Why Learn German?*, Goethe Institute)

Exercise 9 Looking at Cartoons

➤ Working with Cartoons (SB, p. 225)

a Describe cartoon 1, ↑ using the following checklist.
1 Where does the cartoon take place?
2 What situation does it show?
3 What does the cartoon imply?
4 Look up any words which you do not know.

b Analyse and comment on cartoon 1. ↑
1 Is the cartoon topical? If so, what does it refer to?
2 Are the figures in the cartoon shown positively or negatively? How is this done?
3 Does the cartoon use irony? If so, what is its effect?
4 Do you think the cartoon is funny? Explain.
5 Is the cartoon effective? Explain.

c Now give a similar short analysis of cartoon 2. →

Mind Mapping

➤ Context Box, SB, p. 108

Exercise 1

➤ Mind Mapping (SB, p. 222)

a Complete the mind map, which has been started for you, with as many of your own ideas as possible. The following terms might help you.

books • quality papers • e-mails • Internet • magazines • news magazines • newspapers • periodicals • radio • specialist magazines • tabloids • TV

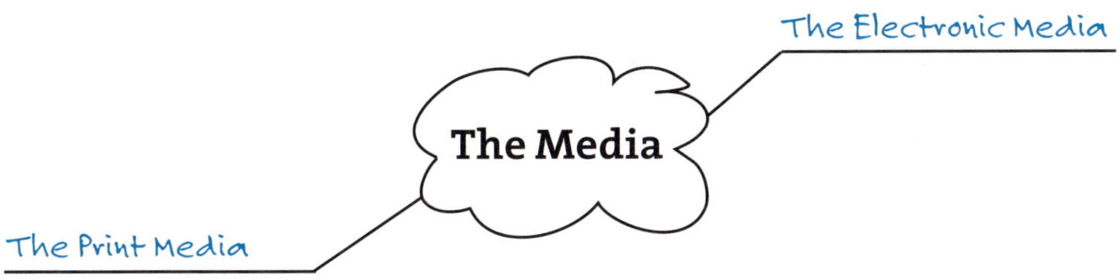

b Read through the short sketches of publications from Britain and the USA. Then choose three of the German publications listed in the box and describe them in the same way for an English-speaking person.

- The *New Statesman* is a British left-wing weekly magazine which deals with topical political issues.
- The *Washington Post* is a US daily which is one of the country's leading quality newspapers.
- The *Sun*, owned by Rupert Murdoch, is Britain's biggest tabloid daily. It has a reputation for sensational reporting.

Bild • *FAZ* • *Neues Deutschland* • *Der Spiegel* • *taz* • *Die Zeit*

1 ____

____

2 ____

____

3 ____

____

Exercise 2

Who Supports What?

➤ Context Box, Texts 1A–D, SB, pp. 108–112

a Using the information in the tables, say whether you agree with the statements below.

Papers and Politics

(From: James O'Driscoll, *Britain*, OUP, Oxford, 1995)

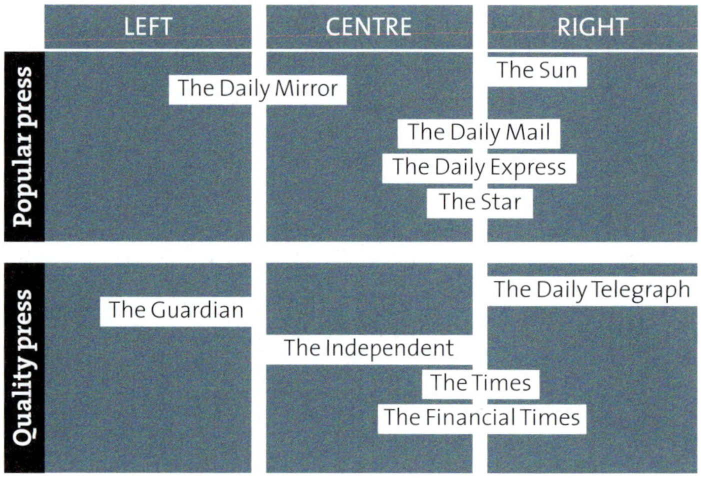

Circulation*

Popular press:	
The Sun	3,569,000
The Daily Mail	2,387,000
The Daily Mirror	2,263,000
The Daily Express	1,062,000
The Star	613,000
Quality press:	
The Daily Telegraph	1,031,000
The Times	722,000
The Financial Times	459,000
The Guardian	395,000
The Independent	224,000

*number of copies sold each day

	Agree	Disagree
1 Most British people are right-wing, supporting the Conservatives.	■	■
2 Owners of British newspapers tend to be Conservative supporters.	■	■
3 When people in Britain buy a newspaper, they are not only interested in the paper's political sympathies.	■	■
4 More people read tabloids than quality papers.	■	■
5 British newspaper readers are more interested in well-researched facts.	■	■

b Invent headlines from the *Guardian* and the *Sun* for the events below.

1 The England football team have beaten Germany in the World Cup.

____

2 The British government is holding a referendum on whether to join the euro.

____

3 A well-known TV star, John Leslie, is accused of forcing a young actress to have sex.

____

Exercise 3

Inventing the Facts

➤ Texts 1A–D, SB, pp. 109–112

Fill in the gaps in the article on the opposite page. Use only the words in the box below and in the form in which they are given.

articles • coverage • editor • exposed • hacker • journalists • magazine's • quality • sensational • source • taken up

Earlier this month the ________________ (1) US newspaper, the *New York Times*, fired 27-year-old journalist Jason Blair on discovering that he had used material stolen from another ____________ (2) in one of his ____________ (3). Six ________________ (4) then had to go through the 725 pieces that Blair had written since 1998 to check that he had not invented other facts. However, Blair was an amateur compared with Stephen J. Glass, a successful young assistant ______________ (5) on the *New Republic*, who started a campaign of dishonest reporting. He invented an imaginary teenage ______________ (6) who uses the Internet and backed up his __________________ (7) stories with interviews which had never taken place. His ______________ (8) of a story about a Church of George W. Bush in Texas and a company that worshipped[1] Alan Greenspan, the head of the Federal Reserve Bank, were eagerly ______________ (9) by other journalists. The ________________ (10) management, Glass recalls, 'loved me' – until his 'scoops' were ________________ (11) as a pack of lies.

[1] worship sb./sth. *jdn./etwas anbeten*

(Based on the article 'When Journalists Lie, They're Fired. If Politicians Lie, They Go to War', *Guardian Weekly*, 22–28 May, 2003, p. 22)

A Letter to the Editor

➤ Text 1E, SB, p. 114

Exercise 4

➤ Writing Letters (SB, p. 250)

a Read the following points to help you when writing a letter to the editor. Information on how to start and end a letter to the editor is given in the Skills Pages in the SB.

- Do not write too much – long letters will be cut, and the editor may then leave out arguments you think are important.
- Write clearly and concisely, giving brief examples to support your argument.
- Remember that your main aim is to convince your readers that you are right.

b Now write a letter to the editor, commenting on one of the following fictitious articles (all of the items refer to events in well-known songs):

Sailor Sues Royal Navy For 'Inhuman Treatment'

A 24-year-old sailor is suing the Navy for spraying water on him with a hosepipe after he was found drunk on board ship. 'They even made a song about me,' he complained.

Farmer Fined For Having 'Too Many Animals'

Farmer Angus Macdonald, aged 68, has been fined by the Department for Environment, Food and Rural Affairs for having 'too many different kinds of animals' on his farm. This goes against EU guidelines which state that in order to prevent disease small farms must not have more than five kinds of animals. Supporters of the farmer are organizing a protest and have even composed a protest song, 'Old Macdonald Had a Farm'.

Red-nosed Rudolph Lights Santa's Way

One of Santa Claus's reindeer, who had usually been kept off the Christmas reindeer team because of his large shiny red nose, got a nice surprise this Christmas when fog suddenly hit the northern hemisphere. Santa Claus decided to ask him to lead the team through the skies because he could then see much better in the foggy skies. When interviewed after a hard night's work, Rudolph said, 'It was fantastic. I've been discriminated against for so long by all the other reindeer, it was thrilling to be able to do something to fight back and take my rightful place on the team. Only one small jump for me, maybe, but it was a huge leap for the Red-Nosed Reindeer Anti-Discrimination Movement.'

Exercise 5

Bad News

➤ Texts 1A–D, SB, pp. 109–112

Underline the correct alternatives in the following news item.

The news from the US **are • is** bleak. **Billion • Billions** of **dollar • dollars** have been wiped off share prices as Wall Street **reel • reels** under a crash which many people are comparing with October 1929. One firm alone lost **ten billions of dollars • ten billion dollar • ten billion dollars** in one afternoon. The US **are • is** currently going through an economic crisis caused by excessively high government deficits and a slump in consumer spending. Although **crisis • crises • crisises** like this are nothing new on world markets, the collapse **has • have** hit Wall Street confidence hard.

Exercise 6

Just Watching

➤ Texts 2A–C, SB, pp. 115–117

a The German word *Zuschauer* has several English equivalents, which are listed in the box below. Select the correct words to complete the sentences on the opposite page. The words can be used more than once.

audience • onlookers • spectators • viewers

1 Many _______________ have written in to the BBC to ask for a second chance to see this film.

2 The _______________ cheered when Chelsea scored in the 89th minute.

3 'What a boring _______________ you are tonight,' the comedian said.

4 A crowd of _______________ gathered at the scene of the bank robbery.

5 Several _______________ were injured when one of the Grand Prix cars ploughed into a crash barrier.

6 TV stations have to give the _______________ what they want.

7 A member of the _______________ had a heart attack during the performance of Tchaikovsky's Swan Lake at Covent Garden.

b Now write four sentences of your own which include each of the words in the box.

Debating

Exercise 7

➤ Debating (SB, p. 252)

a In a formal debate it is important to have strong arguments which are presented convincingly and in their order of importance. Prepare for a debate on the topic 'The Internet needs to be regulated' by writing out at least three arguments for *or* against the motion. Remember, it does not matter what you really think about the topic, but rather how persuasive your arguments are. Use the guidelines given in the Skills Pages in the SB to further prepare for your debate.

b Carry out a debate in class on the topic above. Divide into teams according to which position you have taken. Compare and organize your arguments before you start. The phrases below will help you.

Ladies and gentlemen, I would like to propose the motion that ...
There are many good reasons for agreeing with this ...
First(ly) ..., second(ly) ..., third(ly) ..., finally ...
Ladies and gentlemen, on behalf of my team I wish to oppose the motion that ...
Ladies and gentlemen, I wish to second the motion that ...
I would like to support my team's rejection of the motion ...
It is undeniable ...
There can be no doubt ...
Most observers would agree that ...
In conclusion, ladies and gentlemen, we believe that ...
If I may summarize briefly my team's main points, these are ...

Exercise 8

➤ The Definite Article (*Cornelsen English Grammar*, §§ 182–188)

Selling Articles

➤ Texts 4A–B, SB, pp. 120–122

Correct any mistakes in the use or non-use of the definite article in the text below.

It is a well-known fact that the industry tries to manipulate the consumer behaviour by advertising. In its early days the advertising was simply intended as a means of providing information about products which manufacturers wanted to sell. Once people's basic needs were satisfied, the advertising industry began to look for new fields to operate in. The 1960s consumer society encouraged the expansion of the advertising, so that its function could be described as manipulation of the consumers so that more consumer goods would be consumed. Nowadays the most consumers have swallowed this propaganda. The people do not like to think that they cannot afford the latest toys which the industry is trying to sell them, and when the advertising shows them pictures of slim, young, healthy people eating chocolate which will make them fat, they are only too willing to fall into the advertisers' trap.

'That's a crazy idea but it might work.'

Exercise 9

Brave New World

➤ Texts 4A–B, SB, pp. 120, 122

Write an advertisement or a short brochure for the futuristic baby-cloning clinic 'KIDS R US'. Keep in mind what you learned from Texts 4A and 4B. The following words and phrases might also be useful:

a perfect product • totally satisfied • designer baby • type of face • level of IQ • talents • high resistance to disease • save money on sth. • health insurance • a money-back guarantee • after sales service • free of genetic defects • yearly instalment(s) • loan • at low interest rates

Warning: WWW = World's Weirdos and Whackos

Exercise 10

Fill in the gaps with prepositions taken from the box. The numbers in brackets indicate the number of times each preposition is used in the text.

about (2) • at (1) • despite (1) • of (4) • on (5) • onto (2) • to (3) • via (1) • with (1)

We rely ________ the media for most of our information ________ world events, whether we listen to the news ________ the radio or watch it ________ TV. Information comes to us ________ all sorts of media, and the electronic media are becoming increasingly important as more and more people learn to download texts ________ their computers. Yet this explosion ________ information is not without its downsides. The huge variety ________ data ________ the Internet is a good example ________ the dilemma we face. The Internet gives us access ________ an enormous number of sources which in the past were inaccessible ________ most people. Yet ________ the same time we have even fewer means ________ checking the reliability of these sources than ________ the traditional media, since we have much less information ________ these sources, and there are virtually no checks ________ who puts information ________ , say, a website. The Internet, ________ its many advantages, is an open invitation ________ the weirdos and whackos of this world.

Exercise 1

Who Are They? ➤ Texts 1A–B, SB, pp. 127–128

a Using the words and phrases below, make a profile of a famous person without naming them. Note that 'they' can be used to refer to somebody when you do not want to say what sex that person is. The vocabulary below will help you with your description.

Examples:
'The person I'm thinking of has short fair hair, hazel eyes and a Roman nose.'
'They have a thin face and are very tall.'

Hair: short • long • shoulder-length / straight • curly • wavy • spiky • straggly / light brown • dark brown • fair • ginger • black • grey • white / bald • getting thin on top
Facial hair: sideburns • moustache • beard • clean-shaven
Face: round • square • thin • chubby
Skin: wrinkles • freckles
Complexion: fair • dark • tanned
Eyes: brown • blue • grey • hazel
Nose: large • small • thick • thin • pointed • Roman
Height: tall • medium height • short
Build: obese • fat • stout • muscular • slim • thin
Age: in his/her twenties, thirties, forties, etc.

b In class, form two teams. Team A has to guess who Team B's descriptions refer to, and vice versa. The teacher acts as umpire and score counter.

c Use your imagination and the vocabulary above to describe one of the characters in Text 1A or 1B, for example the old woman mentioned in Text 1A, line 1.

Exercise 2

Passing through Aziziya ➤ Texts 1A–B, SB, pp. 127–128

These are the notes made by a British journalist while accompanying US troops in Iraq during the 2003 war. Write out his report, taking care to use the right tenses (i.e. past, past perfect and conditional) and to insert any words needed (e.g. the definite article).

5 p.m.
- whole country – seems – burning
- while approaching small town, Aziziya.
- pillars of thick, grey smoke, like tornadoes, reveal Aziziya's position

6 p.m.
- sun just set – rushing through Aziziya in convoy of US marines
- unnatural fires light up town, flickering in hearts of burning trucks, tanks
- in near-darkness can just see ugliness of quick, nasty battle fought here
- to right – scorched row of shops
- on left – truck burning in front of restaurant

6.45 p.m. – our column grinding to a halt
– marine thinks he spotted enemy troops

7 p.m. – turns out to be a false alarm – only two goatherds taking goats home
– set off again
– town dark, but civilian traffic, headlights on, moving through streets
– ambulance, lights flashing, trying to get through US checkpoint

7.30 p.m. – night hot and still
– frogs croaking
– beyond town more fires reflected in pools in date groves
– we see Iraqi tank
– still appears to be moving
– our lead tank fires at it, hits
– tank crashes into ditch.

(Based on a report by James Meek in the *Guardian*, 4 April, 2003, p. 3)

Writing Poems

➤ Texts 2A–C, SB, pp. 131–132

Exercise 3

➤ Glossary: Poetry (SB, p. 256)

The purpose of a poem is to express ideas or thoughts in a compact way using words which carry aesthetic or emotional power, not just in their meaning, but also in their sounds and in the images they suggest. Anybody who has ideas in their head can write a simple poem. Write a short anti-war poem of five to ten lines using free verse like the one by Carl Sandburg on p. 131 of the SB. The vocabulary listed below may be useful.

artillery • bomb • cattle • civilian • corpse • gun • general • medal • rifle • shell • slaughter • slaughterhouse • soldier • trench • wound • youth

Exercise 4

How to Bluff Your Way as a Theatre Buff

➤ Texts 3A–D, SB, pp. 132–134

Imagine you have been to a performance of Macbeth. A theatre enthusiast asks you what you thought of the performance. You feel a little unsure, but as you do not want to seem uneducated, you decide to bluff your way through. Formulate at least four sentences. The vocabulary given in the boxes will help you. Look up any words you do not understand.

'I sensed a fine balance between the misery on the stage and the misery in the audience.'

Example:
I thought the costumes were fantastic, but the sets were a bit shoddy.

cast • costumes • directing • leading lady • leading man • sets

beautiful • excellent • fantastic • good • good-looking • impressive • marvellous • professional • realistic • stunning

amateurish • boring • hopeless • mediocre • plain • poor • shoddy • slow • ugly • unrealistic

Exercise 5

Writing a Film Review

➤ Writing Reports and Reviews (SB, p. 251)

a Read the Skills Page in the SB on writing reviews, then look at the text below, which is adapted from an authentic film review from the London magazine *Time Out*. Which of the elements mentioned on the Skills Page occur in the review? Mark them in the text.

How to Lose a Guy in 10 Days

Director: Donald Petrie

Andie Anderson (Kate Hudson) works for Composure magazine, writing articles on how to have great orgasms, lose weight and be a better person. She'd rather write 'How to bring peace to Tadjikistan' (really!), but a job's a job and her latest project is to prove that by making dating mistakes – acting like a clingy, whining, soft-toy-loving Celine Dion fan – she'll get a guy to dump her. By sheer coincidence her target – cynical advertising man Benjamin Barry (Matthew McConaughey) – has just bet his boss he can find a girl to fall in love with ... in 10 days.

The blurb calls this 'unpredictable'; since Andie isn't eaten by sharks and Benjamin doesn't go off with his best mate Tony, that's a matter of opinion. One suspects Petrie intended his chick-flick to be a cross between 'Sex and the City' and 'When Harry Met Sally', but he's made one more cliché-ridden 'girl meets boy, problems arise, girl gets boy' movie. (Oops, that's just given away the 'unpredictable' ending.)

The talented Hudson gives it her best – she's sexy, funny and very convincing – but she's fighting an uphill battle against one-dimensional characters and a ridiculous plot. Credit for this mush must also go to writers Kristen Buckley and Brian Regan for priceless exchanges like: (Andie) 'Are you trying to kill yourself?' – (Benjamin) 'If that's what it takes, yes!' If you liked Petrie's 'Miss Congeniality', you'll love this.

7 dating (adj) *of a romantic relationship* **7** clingy (infml) *too dependent on another person* **7** whine *complain* **14** blurb *short description of a film, book, etc. written by its makers* **18** chick-flick (infml) *film which appeals to young women* **28** mush (infml) *sentimental rubbish*

(Adapted from: Jan Fuscoe, *Time Out*, 16–23 April, 2003, p. 78)

b Summarize briefly, in one or two sentences, what the reviewer thinks of the film. Quote sections of the review which support your opinion.

c Write a review of a film you have seen recently. Write about 200–250 words.

The Coventry Speech

➤ Texts 5A–B, SB, pp. 137–138

Exercise 6

Imagine you are part of a delegation from Dresden which is visiting Coventry as part of the town twinning programme between the two cities. The head of the delegation, Peter Uecker, asks you to help him to write a short five-minute speech to a group of Coventry city councillors, 'weil mein Englisch so miserabel ist'. The topic of the speech is 'shared suffering, reconciliation and rebirth'. He tells you the main ideas he wants to mention. Base your speech on the following notes in English.

- both cities **suffered**, Coventry 1940, Dresden 1945; ironic that the two main churches destroyed (church = place to worship God, but also Christ's command that 'thou shalt love thy neighbour as thyself')
- encouraging: Coventry and Dresden's **reconciliation** soon after end of war – one of first town-twinning projects Britain-Germany
- **rebirth** of both cities at end of war, but rebirth of the two churches took longer;
  Coventry showed the way – looked to future, turned its back on past, new cathedral completed 1962;
  Dresden took longer: ruins left as reminder of the horrors of war, after German reunification followed Coventry's lead and rebuilt Frauenkirche
- Coventry and Dresden shared horrors of war – both suffered;
  reconciliation and rebirth meant that although the suffering was terrible, it was not in vain;
  the gold orb and cross donated by Britain's Dresden Trust – a symbol of that shared experience of suffering: one of craftsmen who made it was son of a British pilot involved in Dresden raid;
  from suffering to reconciliation and rebirth – a learning process which both cities can be proud of

You could begin like this:

Ladies and gentlemen,
The recent history of our two cities can be summarized as ...

Exercise 7

Habits and Processes

Underline the correct verb forms in the short texts below.

1 Normally people at a concert **are making • make** all sorts of noises. They **are coughing • cough**, or they **are rustling • rustle** with hats or bags, but at the Kulturbund concert there **has been • was** absolute silence during the performance.

2 'What **does that man do • is that man doing**?'
'Which man? Oh, you **mean • are meaning** the conductor. He **seems • is seeming** to **talk • be talking** to the soloist. Maybe she **has • is having** some sort of problem with the microphone. They **are often having • often have • often do have** problems with the technical equipment here, you know. No, I'm wrong. **I'm thinking • I think** she's going to sing an encore. And look over there – the orchestra director **brings • is bringing** her a fantastic bouquet of red roses. **Doesn't it look • Isn't it looking** beautiful?'

3 I **watched • was watching** the bridge in the distance when the old man suddenly **spoke • was speaking** to me. 'I **came • have come** 12 kilometres now – from San Carlos. I **have taken • took • was taking** care of the animals there, but the captain **has told • told** me to leave because of the artillery. I'm worried about the pigeons. I **left • have left** them in the cage.'
'**Have you locked • Did you lock • Were you locking** the pigeons' cage?' I asked. 'No.'
'Then the pigeons **are flying • fly • will fly** away, so don't worry.'

4 A man who **lead • led • was leading** a mule **looked • was looking** back over his shoulder, then he **looked • was looking • did look** up at the sky. Suddenly he **spotted • was spotting • did spot** a plane in the sky. He **shouted • was shouting** to the other refugees. They **have all run • all ran • all were running** for cover.

Exercise 8

➤ Prepositions (*Cornelsen English Grammar*, §§ 246–250)

Watch That Preposition!

➤ Texts 1–4, SB, pp. 127–135

Circle or underline the correct preposition from the alternatives given. Sometimes more than one preposition is correct.

1 I met my husband **at • by • on** a concert twenty years ago.
2 We saw a very funny play **by • from • of** Tom Stoppard last Saturday.
3 When you're actually **at • in • on** stage you'll lose your nervousness.
4 Make sure you get to the theatre **at • by • till** 7 pm or you may not get a ticket.
5 We were stunned **about • at • over** the news of R.S. Thomas's death.
6 I waited outside the cinema **at • for • on** you **by • till • to** 9 pm but you didn't come.
7 Most of the refugees were going **by • on • to** foot because they had no other means of transport.
8 Through my window I can see the poppies blowing **at • in • on** the war cemetery.
9 I hope I can rely **at • for • on** you not to tell me if the film has a happy ending.
10 The audience immediately responded **at • on • to** the music.
11 I want you to hand in this work **by • till • up to** next Thursday.
12 Penny can't come. She's taking care **about • for • of** her sick grandmother.

Can't You Take Criticism?

➤ Watch Your Language, SB, p. 141

Exercise 9

Fill in the gaps with the correct form of the word from the box.

critic • critical • critically • criticism • criticize

1 I think we've got to look at this suggestion ______________ .

2 Siegfried Sassoon and Wilfred Owen were two First World War poets who were among the most outspoken ______________ of the slaughter on the Western Front.

3 If you can't stand being ______________ you shouldn't be in politics.

4 We may not like ______________ but it helps us to see our weaknesses and thus overcome them.

5 Our English teacher is always very ______________ of our work, especially if it contains a lot of spelling errors.

6 Many literary ______________ have claimed that George Orwell's novels are too journalistic.

7 He looked at his girlfriend ______________ when she said she'd never heard of a group called Crazy Crocodiles.

8 At a ______________ stage in the production of the film *My Life As a Shark* the leading man suddenly decided to go off to the Bahamas for two weeks' holiday.

Conflicts and Controversies

Exercise 10

Look at the opinions listed below. Pick one and say why you agree or disagree with it. Give reasons and support your view with examples. Write about 150 words.

'If people in the rich West don't try to change things, who will?'

'Modern art has lost touch with ordinary people.'

'Showing pictures of war victims on TV is immoral.'

'Taxpayers' money should not be wasted on subsidizing the arts.'

'It's no use protesting. We can't change anything anyway.'

Exercise 1

➤ Writing a Comment (SB, p. 249)

What Is Germany?

➤ Lead-in, SB, p. 142

How would you describe Germans and Germany? Write a comment of about 200 words in support of your view. Remember:
– Start with a brief introduction;
– Use one paragraph for each of the main arguments you are presenting;
– Support your arguments with examples;
– Finish with a brief conclusion, summing up your most important arguments.

The following qualities may give you some ideas:

arrogant • boring • conformist • conservative • easy-going • eccentric • emotional • fashionable • fun-loving • good food • good sense of humour • hard-working • keen on culture • liberal • militaristic • nationalistic • polite • pacifist • patriotic • progressive • reserved • serious • stiff • thorough • tidy • tolerant • unreliable

Exercise 2

British

➤ Text 1A, SB, p. 144

a Look at the way the words British, Briton and Brit are described in this excerpt from the *Oxford Advanced Learner's Dictionary*. What does it tell you about how they are used?

WHICH WORD?
British / English / Briton / Brit ?

There is no noun which is commonly used to refer to the people of Britain. Instead the adjective **British** is used: *She's British.* ◇ *The British have a very odd sense of humour.* The adjective **English** refers only to people from England, not the rest of the United Kingdom.

The noun **Briton** is used mainly in newspapers: *The survivors of the avalanche included 12 Britons.* It also describes the early inhabitants of Britain: *the ancient Britons.* **Brit** is informal and can sound negative. **Britisher** is now very old-fashioned.

⇨ note at SCOTTISH

(Note on usage from *Oxford Advanced Learner's Dictionary* [sixth edition])

b Now complete the following sentences with an appropriate word meaning 'person(s) or thing(s) from Britain'.

1 Fish and chips is a type of food which is regarded as typically ______________ .

2 The earliest Roman settlement in London was attacked and burned down in AD 60 by the ______________ .

3 Have you ever met any ______________ ?

4 The newspaper headline said: 'SPANISH TRAIN CRASH KILLS EIGHT ______________'.

5 When I was in Majorca on holiday, I met a lot of ______________ .

6 Some people abroad find it hard to understand us ______________________.

7 Doris, have you heard about that train crash in Spain? Eight ______________________ were killed in it. It was terrible!

Mapping the Immigrants ➤ Text 4C, Context Box, SB, pp. 152, 157

Exercise 3

a On the map of the world below, use arrows to show roughly where the main groups of immigrants to Britain came from in the 20th century. Details are given in Text 4C and in the Context Box. Number the arrows and at the bottom of the map give the following details:

- name of immigrant group;
- area or region of origin;
- dates of immigration (where these are given).

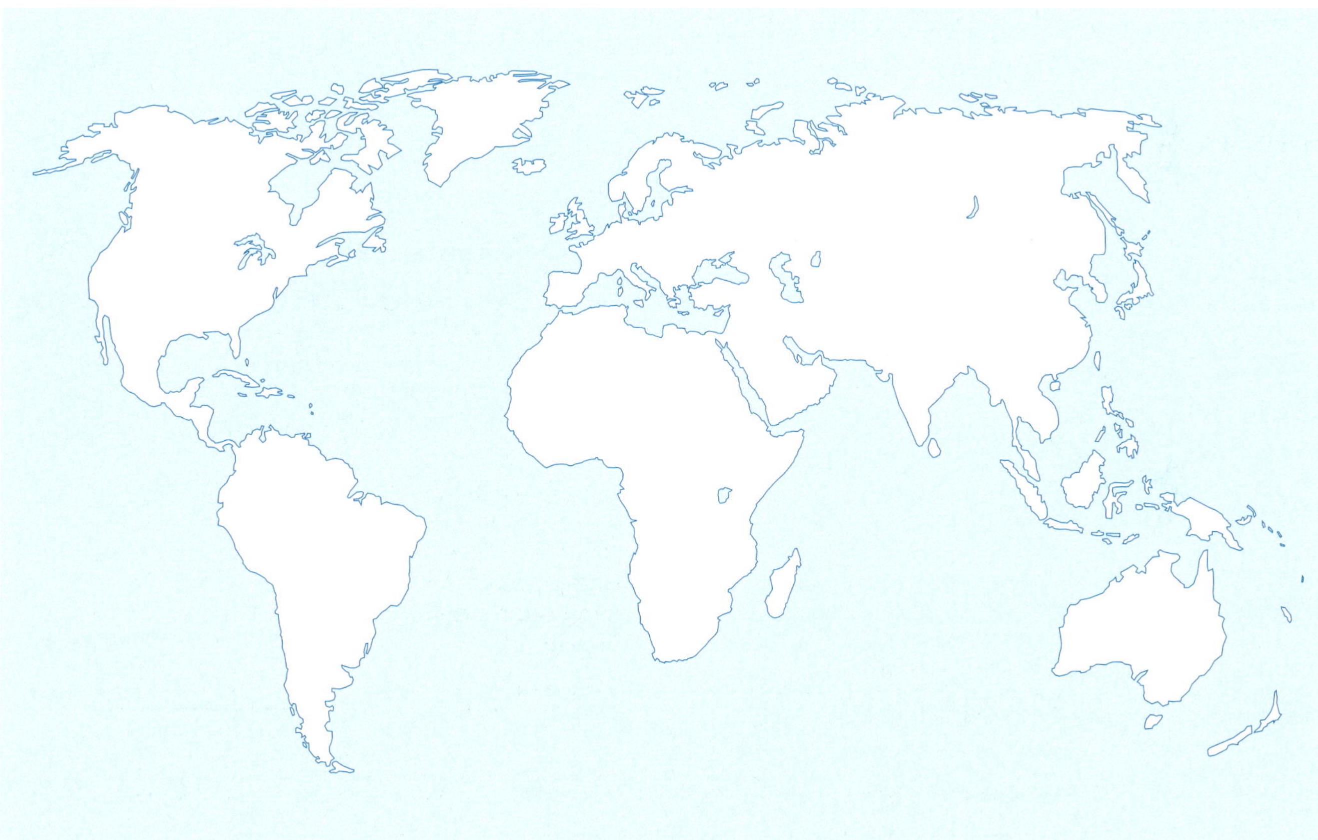

____

____

____

____

____

b In the table below, collect facts about the different ethnic groups mentioned in Text 4C. Notice that the text does not give information for all the boxes.

Ethnic group	Intermarriage: marrying white partners	Economic prospects

Exercise 4

Ethnic Groups

➤ Lead-in, Texts 1A and 4C, SB, pp. 142, 144, 152

a Fill in the blanks in the table with words and phrases referring to national and ethnic groups, some of which are mentioned in the Lead-in and in Texts 1A and 4C. Begin by working out how types A, B and C are different from each other. After filling in the blanks, state which of these types the other words belong to.

Type	**Country**	**Adjective**	**One person**	**Several people**	**Ethnic group**
A	Germany	German	a German	(some) Germans	the Germans
B	England	English	an English person	(some) English people	the English
C	China	Chinese	a Chinese	some Chinese	the Chinese
		British			
	Wales				
			a Scot		the Scots
	France			(some) French people	
	Holland				
	Bangladesh				
			a Jew		the Jews
	India				
	Japan	Japanese			
	Ireland				
	Pakistan				

b Now complete the following text, using words from the table.

London's East End has been the home of one wave of immigrants after another. In the 17th century ________________ Protestants, the Huguenots, came to escape religious persecution in France. They were followed in the early 19th century by ____________ ____________, who came over from Ireland in search of jobs. Then in the second half of the 19th century there was a large influx of ______________ refugees escaping anti-Semitic pogroms in Russia and Eastern Europe. Finally, in the 1960s and 1970s it became the home of thousands of ______________________ from the poor rural area of Sylhet in Bangladesh. Some of the 17th-century Huguenots settled in Soho, which is nowadays better known as the location of London's Chinatown, although in fact most of London's 60,000 ___________________ live outside Soho.

Oh Heribert!

➤ Text 4A, SB, p. 150

Exercise 5

Heribert is not very bright. He is on his first trip to Britain and is a bit confused. Correct his mistakes.

1 'Why are English place names so difficult to understand?'

'Oh, Heribert! That's not an English place name. _______________________ .

2 'Why do some Englishmen wear dresses?'

'Heribert, they're not English, ______________________________ .'

3 'Most Germans don't like English beer, but I do. I'm a big fan of Guinness, for example.'

'Don't you know that Guinness _______________________ ?'

4 'Why does this English £10 note look different from the ordinary ones? Do you think it's a forgery?'
'Heribert, can't you read?
_______________________________________ !'

5 'Why is that Englishwoman wearing a funny hat?'
'Oh Heribert! You're hopeless. She's a _______________.
She's wearing the national costume – probably for tourists like you.'

Exercise 6

➤ Writing Letters (SB, p. 250)

What If?

➤ Texts 6A–B, SB, pp. 158, 160

Imagine what would have happened if the course of history had been completely different: because Europe was weak and backward it was conquered by several big African and Asian states, which divided it up arbitrarily into colonies (see map below). You live in Elberia, a former colony of the African superpower, Yoruba. Yoruba wants to introduce a law which will restrict the number of Elberian immigrants to Yoruba. Write a letter to the editor of the main Yoruba newspaper, *Fitila*, reminding Yorubans of their responsibilities as the former colonial power. Look at the Skills Pages in the SB and the guidelines in this Workbook, p. 39. The notes below might also help you.

You could mention:
- exploitation of Europe by the colonial powers;
- the poverty of most ex-colonies, partly because of neglect by the former colonial rulers;
- the need for Europeans to study and work in African countries, which have more advanced technology and economies;
- ethnic conflict because borders drawn arbitrarily by colonial powers did not take ethnic groups into account.

Conversions

➤ Watch Your Language, SB, p. 163

Exercise 7

➤ Adjectives, Adverbs (*Cornelsen English Grammar*, §§ 196, 203, 205–209)

Rephrase the following sentences, converting the adjective and noun in each sentence into a verb and adverb or adjective, whatever is appropriate. Take special care with the forms of the adjectives and adverbs. Check a grammar book where necessary.

Example:
Your argument isn't very logical.
You aren't arguing very logically.

1 We made a thorough study of the problem. ______

2 This guitar has a pleasant sound. ______

3 Anne's behaviour was very silly. ______

4 The genetic manipulation of humans opens up frightening possibilities. ______

5 They made a lot of money from the illegal sale of drugs. ______

6 He has an eccentric look. ______

7 His actions were extremely cowardly. ______

8 She gave me a furtive look. ______

9 They held a public protest against new anti-immigration legislation. ______

⚠ **Trouble spot**
Watch the adverb of *public* – it is irregular.

10 The linguistic influence of English on Welsh and Irish has been very strong. ______

Exercise 8

➤ Debating (SB, p. 252)

Debate: English for the EU

➤ Text 6C, SB, p. 161

Collect arguments for a debate on the motion 'English should be the official language of the EU'. At least three arguments should be in favour and three arguments against the motion. To help you, read the guidelines given in the SB on debating as well as the hints and phrases given on p. 41 of this Workbook. You may also find the words and phrases below useful.

diplomacy • economic strength • exposed to sth. • global language • military power • political influence • proficient in sth. • supremacy • world power

Exercise 9

Mind the Gap!

➤ Sections 1–6, SB, pp. 144–162

Scan Sections 1–6 in the SB to help you to fill in the gaps with the correct prepositions.

Although Britain has now been a member ________ the European Community, and later the EU, ________ over 30 years, it still shows a strong tendency ________ be sceptical ________ its ties ________ the rest of Europe. One example ________ this is the way people talk ________ 'going to Europe' when they mean the Continent, as if Britain was not part ________ Europe. This approach is typical ________ many people's views ________ the continent on their doorstep. Similarly, the debate ________ whether to join the euro was a reminder ________ Britain's reluctant attitude ________ the EU, and the government's hesitation in holding a referendum ________ the introduction of the euro confirmed this. In any case, many British people see the pound as a symbol ________ Britain's separate identity and are slightly scared ________ the implications ________ Britain's independence which the euro would have.

Going on an Exchange

➤ Lead-in, Texts 1A–D, Context Box, SB, pp. 164–168

Exercise 1

➤ Modal Auxiliaries (*Cornelsen English Grammar*, §§ 22–48)

Fill in the gaps with the English words or phrases which correspond to the German clues given in brackets. If you are unsure, revise modal verbs in your grammar book.

'Dad, my teacher Ms Walker says my marks are so good that next year I ________________ (könnte) go as an exchange student to a school in America. What do you think? ____________ (Darf ich) go, and ________________ (können wir) afford it anyway?'

'I think so, Jenny. It ________________ (dürfte) work out now that I've been promoted. But I'm sure we ______________________ (möchten) find out more about the school before committing ourselves.'

'Well, Ms Walker ______________________ (soll) be arranging a meeting for parents next month. She says our school ____________________________ (konnte) find a second school in the same city which would take exchange students. ________________ (soll ich) ask her if you and Mum ________________ (könnten) make an appointment with her to talk it over? You ______________ (könntet) be able to find out more about things than at a big parents' meeting.'

'Yes, good idea. By the way, when ________________________ (musst du) decide by?'

'We ________________________ (müssen nicht) decide yet, but she ________________ ________________ (möchte) know our final decision by February 21st.'

'She ________________________ (soll) be pretty nice, from what I've heard.'

'Oh Dad, you ________________ (darfst nicht) believe everything you hear. She's okay in general, but sometimes she's a bit moody.'

How We See America

➤ Context Box, Texts 3A–C, SB, pp. 168, 171–172

Exercise 2

a In 2003 the BBC commissioned a survey about how 11 different countries see the United States (including the USA itself). Give your own answers to the questions below, most of which are taken from the 2003 survey.

		yes	no
1	Is your general attitude to America favourable?	☐	☐
2	Would you like to live in the USA?	☐	☐
3	Do you think the worldwide influence of American popular culture (TV, film, pop music, etc.) has a positive effect?	☐	☐

safer | no difference | more dangerous

4 Does America's superior military power make the world a safer place? ☐ ☐ ☐

b Make brief notes, giving reasons for your views:

1 ______________________________

____

2 ______________________________

____

3 ______________________________

____

4 ______________________________

____

➤ Working with Numbers (SB, p. 226)

c In class, collect the answers and formulate them as statistics (e.g. in bar charts). Then compare them with the statistics below on two of the questions from the BBC survey. What similarities and differences do you notice? Speculate about the reasons why the different countries have different attitudes to the USA.

Does America's superior military power make the world a safer place?

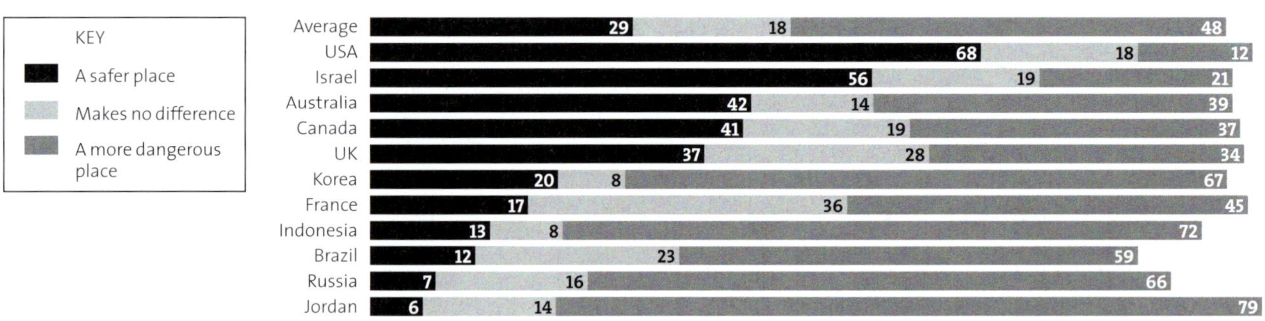

If you had a chance, would you like to live in America?

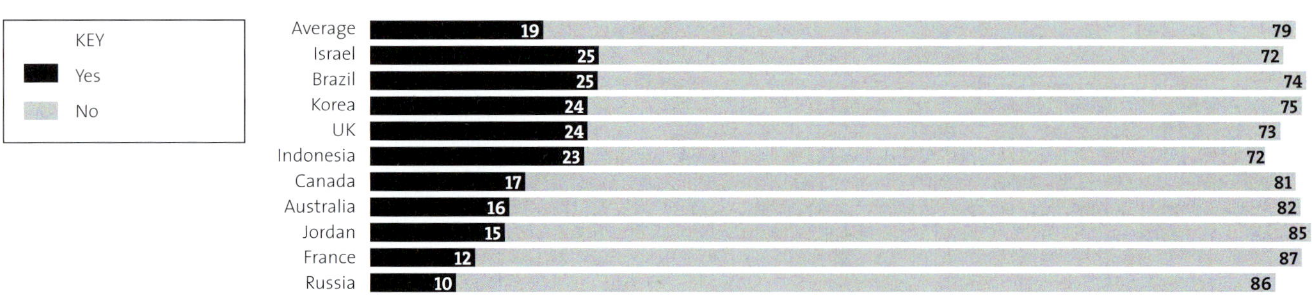

74 % of Americans say they would not like to go and live outside of America if they had the chance and 96% think people outside of America want to go and live there.

(Source: BBC Worldwide)

Choices

➤ Texts 3A–C, SB, pp. 171–172

Exercise 3

Underline the correct word. Sometimes more than one version is possible.

1 Most **countries • lands** in the world have a lower standard of living than the USA.

2 Free access to firearms is a **holy • sacred** cow for the US gun lobby – it doesn't want any restrictions on the availability of guns.

3 New York, which is America's biggest **city • town** with over seven million inhabitants, was only a small **city • town** in 1700.

4 At the battle of Gettysburg in 1863 thousands of men in both the Confederate and Union armies were **killed • murdered • slaughtered** in one of the bloodiest battles during the American Civil War.

5 Not all Americans agree with the US government's **policy • politics** on global warming.

6 When US troops took control of the city, one of the first things they did was to **free • liberate** the prisoners in the jails of the secret police.

7 If we value our **freedom • liberty**, we must remain alert – the state is good at finding reasons for reducing it 'for our own good'.

8 Some Muslim extremists would like to declare a **holy • sacred** war on the USA.

9 It has often been said that **politics • policy** is the art of the possible.

10 The Philippines were only **freed • liberated** from Japanese occupation in the Second World War after many months of bitter fighting.

11 One of the most basic human rights advocated by President Franklin D. Roosevelt in the 1940s was **freedom • liberty** from fear.

How Would You React?

➤ Getting Along in English, SB, p. 177

Exercise 4

You are an exchange student at an American school. How should you react in the following situations? Try to be polite and avoid being blunt. Some of the strategies and phrases on p. 177 of the SB will help you. If you wish, you can also write down what you should *not* say!

1 Somebody in your class at school asks, 'Do people have refrigerators in Germany?'

____

____

2 One of your host family's relatives is visiting. He asks you if Berlin is on the coast.

____

____

3 You are sitting on a park bench next to a 60-year-old man and you start a conversation with him. He tells you that he is a Jew who was born in Germany and lost both his parents in the holocaust. What do you say to him?

____

____

4 A housewife who spent three years in Germany – her husband was in the army – says she loved it there, but could never get used to having to sort out her rubbish and put it in 'four different garbage cans!'

____

____

5 A friend of the host family is telling you about how much she enjoyed her trip to Europe last year. She loved Germany, especially the capital Amsterdam with 'all those canals'.

____

____

Exercise 5

Expressing Opinions

➤ Texts 3A–C, SB, p. 171–172

a Use the flow chart below to state five different opinions you have about the USA and Americans. Briefly say why you take this view and be prepared to support your views with facts, examples, etc. If you wish, you can also use your own expressions.

⚠ **Trouble spot**
I find, in contrast to the German *ich finde*, is only used to express what you have actually experienced.

Example:
I find that the Americans I've met are very interesting.

In my opinion I think (that) My opinion is that I believe (that) In my view I feel (that) My view is that I find (that)	⇨	the USA American pop music US films US foreign policy the Americans I've met US attitudes to the environment US popular culture	⇨	a cultural wasteland arrogant boring cool crazy dynamic easy-going exciting fair fascinating interesting naive nationalistic perfectly normal realistic superficial violent warm-hearted

b After several opinions have been expressed, use the phrases below to comment on what other students have said. Notice that there are some differences in the constructions used.

I regard this idea as ... • I see an opinion like that as ... • I consider this attitude (to be) ... • I view that as ... • I feel ... • I think ...

I Can't Stand Baseball!

➤ Text 5A, SB, p. 178

Exercise 6

Imagine an American friend, who does not speak much German, has seen the text below while staying with you. Since he's keen on baseball, he wants to know what the text says. Summarize it for him in English. Write about 100–130 words. The words and phrases in the box will help you.

annoyed • bat • catcher • home run • obsessed • take sb./sth. seriously

Baseball – ein amerikanischer Volkssport

von Götz Schaller

Ehrlich gesagt konnte ich Baseball nie leiden. Die ganzen Männer, die nichts Besseres zu tun haben, als über eine Sportart zu reden, deren Hauptziel darin besteht, so schnell wie möglich zu laufen, nachdem man den Ball mit einem Stock geschlagen hat, was so ziemlich das ungeeignetste Werkzeug darstellt, um einen Ball halbwegs richtig zu treffen. Am schlimmsten aber sind die Fans, wenn sie von ihren Helden reden: „Weißt du noch, wie Duke Snider damals diesen tollen Home-Run gemacht hat?" Oder: „Pee Wee Reese – das war der beste Catcher, den ich jemals erlebt habe." Wie kann man eine Sportart ernst nehmen, die Spieler mit einem Namen wie „Pee Wee Reese" hervorbringt? Dann gibt es die Fans, die vom Spiel so besessen sind, dass sie sich an jeden Spielzug ihrer Helden erinnern und über das Abschneiden ihrer Mannschaft vor zwanzig Jahren genau so gut Bescheid wissen, als wäre es gestern gewesen. Sie haben zwar keine Ahnung, wie die Hauptstadt ihres Nachbarstaates

Pee Wee Reese

Kanada heißt, aber wer die World Series 1929 gewonnen hat, das wissen sie. Wenigstens ist ihnen bekannt, dass es Kanada gibt, denn da spielen doch die Toronto Blue Jays. Bei Fußballfans – oder, wie die Amerikaner sie nennen würden, „soccer" fans – könnte so was natürlich nie passieren ...

Exercise 7

➤ Relative Clauses (*Cornelsen English Grammar*, §§ 258–266)

Defining or Non-defining?

➤ Text 5B, Watch Your Language, SB, pp. 180, 183

A *defining relative clause* answers the question *Which one?* It defines who or what you are talking or writing about. A *non-defining relative clause* simply gives you extra information about the topic. It does not answer the question *Which one?* Use a relative clause to link up the two sentences given, which are mainly based on Text 5B. Watch the use of commas and relative pronouns. Then tick the appropriate box to show whether the relative clause is defining or non-defining. The first one has been done for you.

defining non-defining

1 Rosey Jekes Café is a nice place to go for cappuccinos.
(where is it?) It's in Anson Avenue.
Rosey Jekes café, which is in Anson Avenue, is a nice place to go for cappuccinos. ☐ ☑

2 The café is called Rosey Jekes Café. ☐ ☐
(which café?) I often go there.

3 The gym is six minutes' walk from her front door. ☐ ☐
(which gym?) She goes to it.

4 Several times a week she goes to the gym. ☐ ☐
(how far?) It's a six-minute walk from her front door.

5 The US spends less than 1% of the budget on pedestrian facilities. ☐ ☐
(which budget?) The budget is used for roads.

6 The US spends less than 1% of its roads budget on facilities for pedestrians. ☐ ☐
(how big?) The roads budget amounts to $25 billion a year.

7 Laconia spent $5 million on pedestrianizing its town centre. ☐ ☐
(where?) Laconia is a town in New Hampshire.

An Ideal Town Centre

➤ Text 5B, SB, p. 180

Exercise 8

➤ Scanning (SB, p. 236)

a Draw a rough plan of your ideal town centre for a small town of, say, 10,000 to 20,000 inhabitants. It may help to scan Text 5B for useful vocabulary. Decide what sort of facilities you would want to have there (cafés, pubs, post office, etc.) and how you would make it attractive for motorists and pleasant for pedestrians. Compare your plans in class. Alternatively, you can draw up a plan for the town you live in.

b Write a short description of your projected town centre. The vocabulary in Text 5B will help you. You may also find the words below useful. Write about 150–200 words.

access • central area • deliver goods • exhaust fumes • pedestrian precinct • pedestrian subways • shopping • speed limit • traffic noise • vehicles

Synonyms

➤ Text 5B, SB, p. 180

Exercise 9

Replace the words underlined by synonyms occurring in Text 5B. Use the space above the word to write your synonym.

1 You should always switch off the car <u>motor</u> if you have to stop at a level crossing.

2 They're a very <u>strange</u> couple. He spends most of his time in the sauna, and she usually wears a fur coat, even in summer.

3 My grandfather hated <u>laziness</u>. He used to say, 'The devil makes work for idle hands.'

4 We are so <u>used</u> to being able to communicate with people whenever we want – by mobile phone, e-mail and via the Internet – that we have completely forgotten that a generation ago none of these existed.

5 I think your idea that we should sell our TV set is absolutely <u>ridiculous</u>. I'd die if I didn't get to see *Friends* every week!

6 We are very <u>worried</u> about the air pollution in our city's streets. We think it's one reason for the rise in asthma cases.

7 The bank robber <u>rushed</u> out of the bank and jumped into the getaway car.

8 Only <u>stupid</u> people would believe the government's claim to be innocent in this corruption scandal.

Exercise 1

Positives, Negatives

➤ Lead-in, SB, p. 184

➤ Glossary: Connotation (SB, p. 266, cf. Diction)

a The words on the left have *positive* connotations, those on the right *negative* ones. Match the corresponding pairs as shown in the example.

assertive	aggressive
calm	arrogant
curious	mean
innocent	naive
quiet	nosy
self-confident	shy
thrifty	unemotional

(calm – unemotional)

b Somebody is describing friends of yours. They obviously don't like your friends and keep using words with negative connotations. Show that you disagree, using words from above meaning the same but with positive connotations. The phrases in the box below suggest different ways of disagreeing. The first response has been done as an example.

I disagree / don't agree ...
I wouldn't call him / say that he's unemotional ...
Do you really think that? I think that's exaggerating.
(I'm afraid) I can't agree with you there, but I admit ...
You can't/don't mean that, surely?

1 'Ben is a terribly shy person, don't you think? He never seems to say anything.'

No, I don't really agree with you. I think he's just a bit quiet, that's all.

2 'Well, I suppose you could say that, but I find him pretty unemotional.

I wouldn't call him unemotional – ______________________________

3 'And he's so naive. The other day I heard him say he didn't think any politician was really dishonest, just misunderstood.'

____

4 'And then there's that friend of his, Alan. He's completely different – a very arrogant person.'

____

5 'What's more, he's so nosy – always poking his nose into other people's business.'

____

6 'And he's mean – he wouldn't lend you money if you were down to your last penny.'

____

Germans or Russians?

➤ Text 1, SB, p. 186

Exercise 2

Complete the text below. Read through the words in the box, which are taken from Text 1, and look up any which you do not understand. Then use them to fill in the gaps in the text.

ancestor • authentic • defiant • demand sth. • ethnic • flourish • give up • humiliate sb. • identity • impostor • persevere • regard sb./sth. • roots • water sth. down

Mixing different ________________ cultures is difficult – not only for the people involved in such relationships. Take the example of ethnic Germans in Russia. Their ________________ were invited there in the 18th century by Catherine the Great. The early years were hard, but only a few ________________ and returned to Germany. Most ________________, gradually building up ________________ German-speaking communities on the Volga and near the Black Sea, where they soon put down ________________. Because they ________________ preserved their way of life, the Russians continued to call them 'Germans'. After the German invasion of the Soviet Union in 1942 they were often ________________ and called 'Fascists'. Many people in the USSR ________________ revenge for their suffering during World War II, and the German minority was often discriminated against. In the 1970s and later many of them emigrated to Germany, where they were now ________________ as Russians. In fact, many of the younger generation by now only spoke Russian. Both in Russia and Germany they have been made to feel like ________________, as if they were ________________ versions of '________________ Germans', or 'real Russians', but in fact they are simply people with a mixed ________________. We ought to see them as *both* German *and* Russian, rather than one *or* the other.

Supermacho

➤ Context Box, SB, p. 189

Exercise 3

Hispanic superhero Supermacho is having identity problems. He goes to his psychiatrist, Dr Joe Headshrinker, for advice. Using the clues given in brackets and the Context Box, work out what advice the psychiatrist gives him.

Headshrinker: Good morning, Mr Fernandez. What can I do for you?
Supermacho: Dr Headshrinker, I've got a problem. My real name is Supermacho. I'm a superhero. The problem is, the other superheroes – Superman, Batman, Captain America, the X-Men – just won't take me seriously. They even call me 'Captain Tortilla' and 'Supernacho'. It's so depressing.

H: Don't let it get you down. ...
(often jealous) (not ashamed – ethnic background)(Hispanic Americans look up to) (someone – to identify) (proud – unique background, upbringing)
S: Right, but it's not just that. They make fun of my partner, Pepe. He helps me in the fight against crime, but they keep saying we're gay.
H: It's usually best to take no notice of that sort of talk. ...
(probably jealousy) (superheroes often lonely) (frequently no stable heterosexual relationship) (rumours – gay – Batman and Robin)
S: Well actually, I am gay, though Pepe doesn't know it.
H: Mr Fernandez, my diagnosis is that you seem ...
(identity crisis) (not the only gay person) (don't choose – sexual orientation) (don't let self-doubts – prevent – realize full potential) (take pride – abilities – help others – fight crime) (don't reduce – complex personality – one feature)
S: Well thanks, Professor, I'd never looked at it that way before.
H: Before your next appointment, ...
(read – self-help book How to Empower Yourself*)*
(help – get your priorities right)

... In addition, I would recommend you to join the Superheroes Anonymous therapy group. You'll probably find that Batman and the X-Men go there, too ...

Exercise 4 Analysing a Video Clip

➤ Text 2A, SB, p. 190

➤ Viewing Skills (SB, p. 267)

a Fill in the viewing log for the video extract of Text 2A. An example is given in the Skills Pages.

Scene	Who?	What?	When?	Where?	Camera work	Comments

b Compare your log with the screenplay. Why did the director use the camera shots chosen?

Writing a Reference ➤ Texts 4C, SB, p. 197

Exercise 5

➤ The Adverb (*Cornelsen English Grammar*, §§ 214–215)

➤ Linking Ideas (SB, p. 246)

Imagine you are a teacher. Write a reference for somebody in your class, using words from the boxes below where relevant. Make sure you put the adverbs in the right position in the sentence. Your fellow students should then try to guess which student the reference describes. Remember that references always stress a person's positive characteristics and abilities. Improve the style of your reference by using connectors.

usually normally often always never late extremely very consistently well also	come to class take part in extra-curricular activities, e.g. sport get on well with fellow students in his/her part-time job speak several foreign languages take part in class work prepare for class	active(ly) conscientious(ly) efficient(ly) fluent(ly) friendly neat(ly) pleasant(ly) polite(ly) punctual(ly) reliable, reliably

Example:
X normally comes to class punctually …

Speculations ➤ Texts 4D–E, SB, p. 198

Exercise 6

➤ Conditional Sentences (*Cornelsen English Grammar*, §§ 251–257)

Life is full of occasions when we wonder what will or would happen if …, and what would have happened if … . Complete the following sentences, taking care to use the correct tense.

1 If I hadn't come to this school, __________

2 I'll leave home unless __________

3 If I were(n't) an only child, I __________

4 Unless I get married, my Mum __________

5 I would've been annoyed if we __________

6 I can use Dad's old car provided __________

7 If I'd been born a century ago, __________

8 If I lived in Palestine, __________

9 I won't be able to go to university unless __________

10 My friends would be surprised if __________

11 If I get the job I want, __________

12 She'd have been offered the job provided the interview __________

____

Exercise 7

Expressing Opinions

➤ Getting Along in English, SB, p. 194

What would you say in the following situations? Use the phrases in the boxes, taking into consideration the situation in each case. Only use each phrase once. In each case, add a sentence explaining briefly why you take this view.

Agreeing
1 I agree (entirely).
2 That's (quite) right/true.
3 I can't agree with you more!
4 Absolutely!
5 You're dead right! *informal*
6 I'm with you there. *informal*
7 That's my view exactly. *formal*

Disagreeing
1 I don't agree (at all).
2 (I'm afraid) I disagree.
3 That's not the way I see it.
4 (Unfortunately) I can't agree with you.
5 You must be joking! *informal*
6 You can't be serious! *informal*
7 Rubbish! *informal*
8 (I'm afraid) I can't accept that. *formal*
9 (I'm sorry,) I don't share your view. *formal*

Admitting that you are wrong
1 Yes, sorry, I think you're (quite) right.
2 You may/might/could (well) be right (about that).
3 You do have a point (there).
4 Silly me! Of course you're right. *informal*
5 I must admit, I think you're right. *formal*
6 Yes, I didn't take that into account. *formal*

1 You're out clubbing with a friend. Your friend says: 'This place is brilliant, isn't it?' You agree, saying:

____

____

2 Your company wants to expand. A colleague has just suggested doing this by exporting more to China. Your boss says: 'I think Peter is quite right. The Chinese market is very promising.' You disagree, saying:

____

____

3 At your host school in the US you've been telling your class something about Germany. Without thinking, you tell them that Germany was reunified in 1871. The teacher in your class says: 'Surely Germany was reunified in 1990?' You admit that you were wrong, saying:

____

____

4 A Scottish friend says: 'I think it's high time compulsory military service was abolished in Germany.' You agree, saying:

____

____

5 At an interview for a holiday job, one of the interviewers says: 'We think it is very important that all our employees are neatly dressed and punctual at all times. What do you think?' You agree, saying:

6 At the same interview, you say that knowing English is not important for the job. One member of the interviewing panel objects, saying that their firm sometimes has visitors from abroad who need to be shown round. You admit that you were wrong, saying:

7 Your English penfriend smiles at you and says: 'You do realize that England will wipe the floor with Germany in the next European Cup, don't you?' You disagree, saying:

8 A reporter for a local newspaper in the US says: 'Many people here think that Europe is not supporting the US enough in fighting against terrorism.' You disagree, saying:

Tense Watching

➤ Watch Your Language, SB, p. 199

Exercise 8

Use the items given to form one sentence. Watch the tenses.

Example:
ever since / I / meet / Andrea / in 1999 / I / be / in love with her
Ever since I met Andrea in 1999 I've been in love with her.

1 ever since / we / buy / this car / last year / it / be / unreliable

2 I / be worried / ever since / Mary / tell me about her son's illness

3 ever since / the computer / be invented / people / become / more and more dependent on it

4 she / be / dissatisfied / since / she / start work / at the supermarket

5 ever since / we / know them / they / complain about the neighbours

____

6 since / he / hear about Kay's promotion / he / be / jealous of her

____

7 I / be / allergic to Chinese food / since / I get / diarrhoea after a Chinese meal two years ago

____

____

Exercise 9

My Ideal Partner

Write five sentences each about the personality and interests of your ideal partner, selecting these from the boxes below. Use the verbs given, arranging them in order of importance as follows:

- essential: *must*
- preferable: *should*
- possible: *can*
- unnecessary: *doesn't have to*
- unacceptable: *mustn't*

'Gerald, I don't think our both being left-handed is enough.'

➤ Linking Ideas (SB, p. 246)

Make your style more fluent by using connectors (see the Skills Pages in the SB).

Personality
adventurous • affectionate • arrogant • conservative • considerate • cool • conventional • easy-going • fashion-conscious • fun-loving • have a sense of humour • intelligent • liberal • outgoing • reliable • religious • romantic • self-confident • serious • shy • tidy • tolerant • untidy

Interests
children • clubbing • countryside • cycling • dancing • films • folk music • going to pubs • jazz • motorcycling • opera • partying • pop music • reading • sport • theatre • travel • watching TV

Example:
Although my ideal partner must be fashion-conscious, she should also be fairly easy-going. In addition, she can enjoy going to pubs. On the one hand she doesn't have to like jazz, but on the other hand she mustn't like folk music.

Describing a Photo

➤ Lead-in, SB, p. 200

Exercise 1

➤ Working with Pictures (SB, p. 223)

a Describe the photo, paying attention to both the foreground and the background. Why is the background not sharply focused?

b The girl in the picture is doing a gap year between school and university in New Zealand. Speculate on what she was thinking when the photo was taken. Write about 50–60 words.

What If?

➤ Texts 1A–C, SB, pp. 202–205

Exercise 2

➤ Conditional Sentences (*Cornelsen English Grammar*, §§ 251–257)

Speculate on the following situations based on Texts 1A–1C. Use conditional sentences.

a Gemma is having problems preparing to run away from home.

1 'Should I write them a note or not? I wonder what would happen if I didn't write them one. I suppose if I ______

2 'Hell! I can't find Dad's Visa card. Unless I ______

3 'I'm glad I didn't write anything nasty in the note, like "How can you bear to live with yourselves after you've made my young life so unbearable?" I'm sure that if I ______

4 'Mum and Dad make me so angry. They won't let me have a life of my own. If only they ______

b Lauren is thinking about what her parents said. Complete her thoughts:

1 'Mum said I might get raped or murdered if ______

2 'If I'd been alive in the sixties ______

3 'Dad asked where I would get the money for university if I ______

4 'What about a trip to Europe? Maybe I'd have more fun if ______

c Laurie Lee is wondering what would have happened if things had turned out differently:

1 'If my mother had tried to persuade me to stay, what ______

2 'I might not have left home if ______

3 'Supposing I'd stayed at home, perhaps I ______

4 'Probably I would have turned back on that first day if ______

Exercise 3

Expanding Your Vocabulary

➤ Text 3, SB, p. 217

Complete the following table containing words which refer to the emotions.

adjective	abstract noun
happy	happiness
elated	
confused	
	respect
melancholy	
depressed	
wise	
	distress
angry	
	violence

Analysing a Cartoon

Exercise 4

➤ Working with Cartoons (SB, p. 225)

Look at the cartoon and answer the questions below.

'We've been thinking a lot about what we want to do with your life.'

1 What is the subject of the cartoon?

2 Describe the important details in the cartoon.

3 Explain the point that the cartoonist is trying to make. How is this done?

Applying for a Job

➤ Text 2A, SB, p. 209

Exercise 5

Your friend Dirk wants to apply for a job in Britain. He has written his CV and a covering letter (cf. next page), but his English is not very good, and he has never written a CV before. He has asked you to correct them for him. Rewrite both, correcting his mistakes. The CV and the 'Useful words and phrases' on p. 210 of the SB will help you.

CV for Dirk Meiningen, Adelsbergstraße 24, 09126 Chemnitz

Birth date:	9 octobre 1986
Languages:	English, French, some Czech
Hobbys:	football, chess, computer, travelling
Education:	
1987-1992	Rosa-Luxemburg-kindergarden
1992-1996	Ernst-Moritz-Arndt-Grundschule
1996-	Goethe-Gymnasium
Qualifications:	I take my Abitur in July 2004 in Maths, Chemistry, English, Sociologie
Experience:	Summer jobs at Macdonalds, at the Krankenhaus Rabenstein, at the restaurant Zum Fröhlichen Sachsen
Date:	16 July 2003
Signature:	Dirk Meiningen

➤ Writing Letters (SB, p. 250)

Dirk Meiningen
Adelsbergstr. 24
09126 Chemnitz

Chemtech Laboratories
12 Parkview Way
Bristol
BS7 1BQ

Chemnitz, 16 july 2003

Re: work placement

Dear Mr Batsford,

after having made my Abitur in june 2004 I want to study chemistry at the University of Mannheim. Before I am going to study I will spend some time doing a work placement, preferably in England. A friend of me said me that I could perhaps do one in your firm. So, I want to ask if you like to take me during the summer of 2004.
You see from the CV I am sending with that I had experience in several jobs. I also take Chemistry for my Abitur, so I think, your firm will be a good place for me.
I look forward to hear from you soon.
Thank you that you consider my application.

With friendly greetings

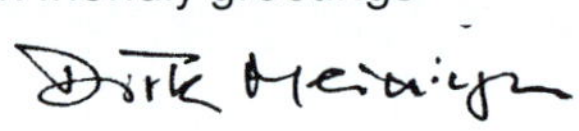

Exercise 6

Sorry, Didn't Quite Catch That

➤ Getting Along in English, SB, p. 216

You are phoning about a room you would like to rent. Unfortunately you do not always understand the woman who answers the phone. Complete the conversation on the opposite page, using the phrases given in the boxes to get her to repeat things and to check whether you understood correctly what was said.

a Asking for repetition

1 Sorry, I didn't hear you.
2 I'm afraid I didn't (quite) catch that.
3 Sorry, it's a bad line. (on the phone)
4 Could you repeat what you said / that last word, please?
5 What was that again? *informal*
6 I'm (very) sorry, would you mind repeating that, please? *formal*
7 Could I ask you to repeat that, please? *formal*

b Checking that you have understood

1 Does that mean …?
2 Am I right in thinking/saying that …
3 I'm not sure I understand. Does that mean …
4 So is the basic idea that …
5 If I've got it right, then … *informal*
6 So what that boils down to is … *informal*
7 If I understand you correctly, … *formal*
8 Would I be correct in thinking that … *formal*

'Hello, I'm phoning about the room in Hackney advertised in today's paper. Does it have central heating?'

'Hello, love. No, just a ... (reply can't be heard due to crackling and hissing on the line).'

'____'

'I said, no, just a gas fire. It's very warm though.'

'And how much is the rent?'

'It's ... (speaks fast and unclearly so that you're not sure what she said).'

'______________________________________, it's £318 a month.'

No, love, what I said was ... (inaudible due to crackling and hissing on the line).'

'____'

'Of course, love. It's £380 a month. Dreadful prices, rooms round here, you know.'

'I see. £380. Does that include heating?'

(Reply can't be heard again due to the bad line.)

'I'm awfully sorry. ____'

'Ooh, it is a bad line, isn't it? I said, no, the heating's extra.'

'______________________________ that the bathroom and kitchen are shared?'

'Yes, love, there are five other people sharing, but they're all very nice, and most of them are very clean.'

Writing an Informal Letter

➤ Context Box, SB, p. 208

Exercise 7

➤ Writing Letters (SB, p. 250)

Pretend that you are the sister of the girl in the cartoon in Exercise 3 (p. 73). Write your parents a letter saying why your sister left home. Some words and phrases (mainly from the Context Box) are listed below to help you.

dependent on sb./sth. • get along on your own • get away from your parents • have a bit of freedom and privacy • rush into marriage • what we want to do with our lives

Exercise 8

Emotional Ups and Downs

➤ Text 3, SB, p. 217

Use the adjectives given to show increasing degrees of emotion in the situations described below. The texts describe how emotions become more intense as the situation develops.

a elated • excited • glad • happy

Eveline was ______________ when she met Frank. He seemed kind, and helped her to cope with her father's bad moods. As their relationship developed, she gradually found herself ______________ for the first time since her childhood. She was ______________ about the new experience of going out with a man, and this reached a climax when he took her to see a play. She felt ______________ to be sitting with him in a part of the theatre where she would not normally go.

b anguished • melancholy • mournful • unhappy

Eveline was tired of being ______________ but the sounds of the city conspired to make her feel depressed. In the distance she could hear a street organ playing a ______________ tune – the same tune that an Italian organ-grinder had played as her mother lay dying. When they got to the station she saw the great black mass of the boat and heard its ______________ whistle. As the time to leave approached, her mood gave way to ______________ desperation as she frantically tried to choose between duty and happiness.

c angry • annoyed • furious • upset

Quietly, Eveline entered the kitchen. Her father was sitting at the table, stoney-faced: 'Do you have any intention of cooking a meal for your father?' he said. At first Eveline was merely ______________ at her father's tone. She felt misunderstood. When the meaning of his words sank in, she noticed how ______________ he was. Her thoughts returned to Frank and the future she had now denied herself. She saw her father before her, wallowing in his selfishness, and became ______________ . When he then told her how ungrateful she was, carrying on with men behind his back, she suddenly grew ______________ . Without realizing what she was doing, she lifted the heavy cast-iron frying pan and hit him with it. When the police arrived, she was still sobbing.

Exercise 9

➤ Expressing Future Time (*Cornelsen English Grammar*, §§ 95–100)

Futures ➤ Watch Your Language, SB, p. 221

Underline the correct forms in the sentences below. In the space on the right, state whether each form refers to *intention*, *prediction*, a *fixed plan*, a *timetable*, or a *spontaneous decision*. Sometimes more than one version is correct.

1 'Have you any idea how this DVD player works?'
'Hang on a minute. **I'll show • I'm going to show** you.' ____________________

2 'What **will you be • are you going to be** when you grow up?' ____________________
'A sailor.'

3 'What **do you do • are you doing** tomorrow?' ____________________

'**I'll go • I'm going** skiing. Fancy coming along?' ____________________

4 'I expect **we'll go • we're going** on holiday to Spain again this year.' ____________________

5 'My plane **leaves • is leaving** at 5.30 pm from Heathrow.' ____________________

6 'The weather tomorrow **will be • is** cloudy, with sunny periods.' ____________________

7 'This film is very sad. I think **I'm going to cry • I'll cry**.' ____________________

8 'There's been an accident.'
'How awful. **I'll phone • I phone** for an ambulance.' ____________________

Exercise 10

➤ Adverbs (*Cornelsen English Grammar*, §§ 214–215)

Alternatives ➤ Texts 3, SB, p. 217

The following sentences are taken from Text 3. Put the adverbs in brackets in the correct position, marking this position in the text with an arrow. In many cases, more than one position is correct.

Example:
He could ↑ be very nice. (sometimes)

1 Ernest never played: he was too grown up. Her father used to hunt them in out of the field, but little Keogh used to call out when he saw her father coming. (often, usually)

2 He is in Melbourne. (now)

3 She gave her entire wages. (always)

4 He used to meet her outside the Stores and see her home. (every evening)

5 When he sang about the lass that loves a sailor, she felt pleasantly confused. (always)

6 She looked round the room, reviewing all its familiar objects which she had dusted once a week for so many years. (regularly)

7 One day he had quarrelled with Frank. (violently)

Assessing Your Level in English

Name: Luisa Bayer

I Learning English so far

1 Where and how have you learned English so far?
(Tick [√] all the answers that apply.)

- [x] in the classroom
- [x] doing homework
- [x] listening to songs
- [x] listening to the radio
- [ ] watching films
- [ ] reading books or magazines
- [ ] speaking with foreigners
- [ ] watching TV
- [ ] other: ____________________

2 These are the areas I feel comfortable and confident in when I use English:

3 These are the areas I think I need to work on:

II Working with the First Part of 'Land/scape' (cf. pp. 8–14)

1 I found the first part of the story

- [ ] enjoyable because
  - [ ] I was curious to see how it would develop.
  - [ ] I could identify with the main character.
  - [ ] I felt it was easy to understand and pleasant to read.
- [x] not enjoyable because
  - [x] it was too difficult to understand.
  - [ ] the subject did not interest me.
  - [x] it was too long.
  - [ ] I don't like reading very much anyway.
- [x] other: I can't understand very much

2 I found the vocabulary used in the story

- [ ] easy to understand and I did not need to look up many words.
- [ ] okay, but I needed to look up quite a lot of words.
- [x] difficult, so I really could not follow the story.
- [ ] other: ____________________

3 I found the sentences in the story

- [ ] relatively simple and easy to understand.
- [ ] tricky, but I was able to follow the story.
- [ ] too long and complicated.
- [ ] other: ____________________

4 I found tasks 1–4 on p. 14

- [ ] easy to answer.
- [ ] useful, as they made me think about the story more.
- [x] too difficult to answer without help from the teacher.
- [ ] other: ____________________

5 During the classroom discussion

- [ ] I joined in a lot.
- [x] I joined in when I knew what I wanted to say.
- [ ] I was unable to express my ideas clearly.
- [ ] I felt uncomfortable talking in English in front of others.
- [ ] other: ____________________

III Working with the Second Part of 'Land/scape' (cf. p. 14)

1 While listening to the text

- ☐ I found it easy to understand what was going on.
- ☐ I could understand the gist of what was happening.
- ☒ I understood very little of what was going on.
- ☐ other: ____________________

2 My main difficulty with the story was the fact that

- ☒ the vocabulary was difficult to understand.
- ☐ the speaker was difficult to understand.
- ☐ the sentences were very long and complicated.
- ☒ the speaker spoke too quickly.
- ☐ other: ____________________

3 The tasks 5–9 on pp. 14–15 were

- ☐ easy to answer.
- ☒ useful, as they made me think about the story more.
- ☐ too difficult to answer without help from the teacher.
- ☐ other: ____________________

4 During the classroom discussion

- ☐ I joined in a lot.
- ☐ I joined in when I knew what I wanted to say.
- ☐ I was unable to express my ideas clearly.
- ☐ I felt uncomfortable talking in English in front of others.
- ☐ other: ____________________

IV Working with the Final Part of 'Land/scape' and with 'Young, Talented and Rebellious' (cf. pp. 15–19)

In tasks 1–6 on p. 19 you and a partner discussed the tasks alternately and then together.

1 When I was talking,

- ☐ I found it easy to express what I wanted to say.
- ☐ I felt uncomfortable speaking in English.
- ☐ I used words from the text to express what I wanted to say.
- ☐ I used my own words when dealing with the tasks.
- ☐ I found my partner's comments useful.

2 When I was listening,

- ☐ I found it easy to understand what my partner was talking about.
- ☐ I just listened to what my partner said until he or she was finished.
- ☐ I made it clear to my partner that I understood him or her and asked questions if I didn't.

You have probably written two short texts – an account of a family trip (p. 17, task 16) and a feature story for your school magazine (p. 19, task 7). Now fill in the questionnaire (You may tick more than one item.):

1 How did you prepare for the actual writing?

- ☐ I wrote down a number of ideas.
- ☐ I organized my ideas to give my text a meaningful structure.
- ☐ I didn't prepare at all, but just started writing immediately.
- ☐ other: ______________________________

2 How did you structure your thoughts?

- ☐ I thought about individual paragraphs, giving each one a title.
- ☐ I created a mind map.
- ☐ I relied on my imagination during the writing process.
- ☐ I did not structure my ideas.
- ☐ other: ______________________________

3 Did you think about possible readers of your texts while preparing or writing?

- ☐ Yes, I tried to consider what they might expect.
- ☐ No, I didn't think about possible readers.
- ☐ Partly, but I was more interested in writing for me.

4 Where did you get the words you used in your text?

- I knew most of the words already.
- My teacher provided me with new words.
- I used my German-English dictionary.
- I used my monolingual dictionary.
- I asked my teacher or friends for words I was unsure about or wanted to use.

5 How did you move from one idea to the next in your text?

- Each idea was given a new paragraph.
- I used quite a number of connectors (e.g. 'firstly', 'therefore', 'on the one hand ..., on the other ...') to move from one idea to the next.
- I didn't always know which connectors to use and when to use them.
- I don't really feel comfortable using connectors, so I left them out.
- I didn't feel that connectors were needed in my texts.

Looking back on the work on the Introduction, I would say my main strengths were:

____

____

____

____

My main weaknesses were: ____________________________

____

____

____

V The Four Skills

1 Reading

a I enjoy reading in English and don't really consider it to be hard work.

- [ ] true
- [x] mostly true
- [ ] not true

It depends: ....

b I can understand letters and e-mails that deal with everyday matters and feelings.

- [x] true
- [ ] mostly true
- [ ] not true

It depends: ....

c I can follow a story with little or no difficulty.

- [ ] true
- [x] mostly true
- [ ] not true

It depends: ....

d I can understand articles and reports that deal with current events and issues and I can recognize the writer's viewpoint.

- [ ] true
- [ ] mostly true X
- [ ] not true

It depends: ....

e I can analyse things I have read for style and literary devices.

- [ ] true
- [ ] mostly true
- [x] not true

It depends: ....

	End of the first term				End of the second term				End of the third term			
	true	mostly true	not true	improved? +/-	true	mostly true	not true	improved? +/-	true	mostly true	not true	improved? +/-
	☐	☐	☐	___	☐	☐	☐	___	☐	☐	☐	___
	☐	☐	☐	___	☐	☐	☐	___	☐	☐	☐	___
	☐	☐	☐	___	☐	☐	☐	___	☐	☐	☐	___
	☐	☐	☐	___	☐	☐	☐	___	☐	☐	☐	___
	☐	☐	☐	___	☐	☐	☐	___	☐	☐	☐	___

2 Speaking

a I can talk about myself, my home and my school with no difficulty.

- [x] true
- [ ] mostly true
- [ ] not true

It depends: ....

b I can talk about current events with little or no preparation.

- [ ] true
- [ ] mostly true
- [ ] not true

It depends: ....

c I can express my opinion and give reasons for it.

- [x] true
- [ ] mostly true
- [ ] not true

It depends: ....

d I can summarize the contents of stories, newspaper articles, films, etc.

- [ ] true
- [x] mostly true
- [ ] not true

It depends: ....

e My pronunciation in English is clear and easy to understand.

- [ ] true
- [x] mostly true
- [ ] not true

It depends: ....

	End of the first term				End of the second term				End of the third term			
	true	mostly true	not true	improved? +/-	true	mostly true	not true	improved? +/-	true	mostly true	not true	improved? +/-
	☐	☐	☐	___	☐	☐	☐	___	☐	☐	☐	___
	☐	☐	☐	___	☐	☐	☐	___	☐	☐	☐	___
	☐	☐	☐	___	☐	☐	☐	___	☐	☐	☐	___
	☐	☐	☐	___	☐	☐	☐	___	☐	☐	☐	___
	☐	☐	☐	___	☐	☐	☐	___	☐	☐	☐	___

3 Listening

a I can follow classroom discussions without any problem.

- [ ] true
- [x] mostly true
- [ ] not true

It depends: ....

b I can understand normal conversation about everyday matters.

- [ ] true
- [ ] mostly true
- [ ] not true

It depends: ....

c I can understand the news on the radio and television and pick out the most important information.

- [x] true
- [ ] mostly true
- [ ] not true

It depends: ....

d I can understand song lyrics.

- [ ] true
- [ ] mostly true
- [ ] not true

It depends: ....

e I can understand different varieties of English (e.g. Received Pronunciation, Northern English, American English, Australian English.)

- [ ] true
- [ ] mostly true
- [x] not true

It depends: ....

	End of the first term				End of the second term				End of the third term			
	true	mostly true	not true	improved? +/-	true	mostly true	not true	improved? +/-	true	mostly true	not true	improved? +/-

4 Writing

a I can write personal e-mails and letters without difficulty.

- [ ] true
- [ ] mostly true
- [x] not true

It depends: ....

b I can write well-structured texts about things I know and care about.

- [ ] true
- [x] mostly true
- [ ] not true

It depends: ....

c I can present information in an essay or report, analysing different standpoints and giving reasons for my own standpoint.

- [ ] true
- [ ] mostly true
- [ ] not true

It depends: ....

d I can write stories and/or poems in clear English and make them interesting to read.

- [ ] true
- [ ] mostly true
- [ ] not true

It depends: ....

	End of the first term				End of the second term				End of the third term			
	true	mostly true	not true	improved? +/-	true	mostly true	not true	improved? +/-	true	mostly true	not true	improved? +/-
	■	■	■	___	■	■	■	___	■	■	■	___
	■	■	■	___	■	■	■	___	■	■	■	___
	■	■	■	___	■	■	■	___	■	■	■	___
	■	■	■	___	■	■	■	___	■	■	■	___

VI Correctness and Comprehension

1 Grammar

a I make very few grammatical mistakes when I'm speaking or writing English, and my mistakes don't lead to misunderstandings.

- ☐ true
- ☐ mostly true
- ☐ not true

b I often make mistakes although I know the rules.

- ☐ true
- ☐ mostly true
- ☐ not true

c I know how to find the correct forms in my grammar book, etc. when I'm not sure of them.

- ☐ true
- ☐ mostly true
- ☐ not true

d I don't have problems with grammatical structures when I read a text.

- ☐ true
- ☐ mostly true
- ☐ not true

2 Vocabulary

a I choose the right words, and my mistakes don't lead to misunderstandings.

- ☐ true
- ☒ mostly true
- ☐ not true

b If I can't think of a word, I can describe what I mean so that other people can understand me.

- ☐ true
- ☐ mostly true
- ☒ not true

c I know how to find words that I need in my dictionary, etc.

- ☐ true
- ☐ mostly true
- ☐ not true

d I can understand most of the words used in texts or guess their meaning from the context.

- ☐ true
- ☐ mostly true
- ☐ not true

	End of the first term				End of the second term				End of the third term			
	true	mostly true	not true	improved? +/-	true	mostly true	not true	improved? +/-	true	mostly true	not true	improved? +/-
	■	■	■	___	■	■	■	___	■	■	■	___
	■	■	■	___	■	■	■	___	■	■	■	___
	■	■	■	___	■	■	■	___	■	■	■	___
	■	■	■	___	■	■	■	___	■	■	■	___

	■	■	■	___	■	■	■	___	■	■	■	___
	■	■	■	___	■	■	■	___	■	■	■	___
	■	■	■	___	■	■	■	___	■	■	■	___
	■	■	■	___	■	■	■	___	■	■	■	___

VII Plan of Action

I have identified these areas of weakness and intend to do the following to improve my English in those areas:

Reading: ____

Plan: I will try to ____________________________________

____

____

Speaking: ____

Plan: I will try to ____________________________________

____

____

Listening: ____

Plan: I will try to ____________________________________

____

____

Grammar: ____

Plan: I will try to ____________________________________

____

____

Vocabulary: ____

Plan: I will try to ____________________________________

____

____

Acknowledgements

Texts

Chapter Five

Ex. 5 Reproduced by permission of Oxford University Press, from *Oxford Advanced Learner's Dictionary* 6th Edition © Oxford University Press 2000.

Ex. 8 From *Warum Deutsch? Why Learn German?*, Goethe-Institut. Reprinted by permission.

Chapter Seven

Ex. 5 From Jan Fuscoe, 'How to Lose a Guy in 10 Days', *Time Out*, 16–23 April, 2003, p. 78.

Chapter Eight

Ex. 2 Reproduced by permission of Oxford University Press, from *Oxford Advanced Learner's Dictionary* 6th Edition © Oxford University Press 2000.

Photos/illustrations

Agentur Focus, Hamburg: pp. 21 (© STEELE HILL / NASA / SCIENCE LIBRARY), 30 (top left, © Network / Mike Goldwater); akg-images, Berlin: p. 14 (all except image 8); Volkhard Binder, Berlin: pp. 51, 54; www.britainonview.com: p. 53 (top right); © British Tourist Authority: p. 53 (top left); www.cartoonbank.com: pp. 46 (© The New Yorker Collection 1998 James Stevenson from cartoonbank.com. All Rights Reserved), 72 (© The New Yorker Collection 2002 David Sipress from cartoonbank.com. All Rights Reserved); Cartoonist & Writers Syndicate, CA / cartoonweb.com: p. 36 (bottom right, © Boligan); www.cartoonstock.com: pp. 27 (© Matt Percival), 42 (© John Morris); Corbis, Düsseldorf: pp. 14 (image 8, © Bettmann), 30 (bottom left, © Don Mason, bottom right, © Corbis SABA / Najlah Feanny), 61 (© Bettmann); Corel-Library: p. 60 (backdrop); dpa-Fotoreport: p. 45 (top, © Romeo Gacad); © Info-Zentrum Schokolade, Leverkusen: p. 30 (top right); The Irish Image Collection: p. 53 (bottom); © Jeongsook Lee, Berlin: pp. 9 (illustrations nos. 1–4), 15, 16; © printing.com, Manchester: p. 36 (top); Private Eye, London: p. 36 (middle, © Copyright Pressdram Limited 2002. Reproduced by permission); © Punch Cartoon Library, London / Michael Ffolkes: p. 70; Posy Simmonds: pp. 3, 4 (© Reprinted by permission of PFD [The Peters, Fraser & Dunlop Group Ltd, London] on behalf of Posy Simmonds / Observer, October 25, 1998); skjoldphotographs.com: p. 71; © Petersen Thomas, Boston: pp. 5, 9 (bottom), 18, 34, 40, 41, 43, 49, 66; US Information Service, Berlin: p. 45 (bottom); © Wales Tourist Board: p. 54 (bottom right; All rights reserved. Unauthorised reproduction of this image is strictly prohibited).